ALL THE GREEN
DISCOVERING GOD'S PLAN FOR YOUR LIFE

CRAIG TUBIOLO

GOD'S PLAN PUBLISHING

PRAISE FOR ALL THE GREEN

Craig Tubiolo in his book "All the Green: Discovering God's Plan for Your Life," comes so very close to answering a number of life's unanswerable questions and those mysteries that are beyond earthly questions much less answers He gives you comfort that all is well in following Jesus Christ teachings even in the most difficult times.

—Joe Estevez
Actor

This book will challenge you to consider the call God has on your life. My dear friend Craig artfully illustrates how a divine point of grace can change the trajectory of our lives as we surrender our plans to His and then begin to walk in His way and for His glory! From Hollywood to film and TV industries and featuring so many stars he's met and interviewed, Craig shares about varying kinds of glory, worldly and divine and how only one can bring us peace, joy and fulfillment.

—Alexis Walkenstein
Author, Producer, Speaker, and Publicist

I heartily endorse "All the Green," not only because of the excellent content geared towards finding true meaning in life in our complex society, but also because I know Craig Tubiolo to be a real man of faith. His interviews with people regarding faith bring out many concrete examples of how people in our world today can deepen their faith and share it with others.

—Bishop Nicholas DiMarzio
Bishop Emeritus of Brooklyn

In "All the Green: Discovering God's Plan for Your Life," author Craig Tubiolo has drawn a clear and inspiring line between the riches of relationship with God and the empty, antiseptic nature of religion. A clear, creative guide to knowing God rather than just knowing about Him, "All the Green" pulls back the doctrinal veil that often shrouds the faith and instead, reveals the heart of a living Lord who loves us so deeply He became a man and poured His life out to make a way to have a love relationship with us. It will both challenge and change anyone who reads it and left me with an understanding of God's plain path to peace, joy, and hope through faith in His love.

—Rick Kern,
Freelance Writer/Editor
Former Pastor and Missionary

Craig Tubiolo Syracusa is a man on a purpose-driven mission. Throughout his career in television, film, and music, he maintains a message of hope in a world mired in despair. Craig's new book will encourage and inspire you to walk in faith. I have known Craig for many years. I have witnessed his compassion for people. He is dedicated to helping people live in the fullness of God's grace. Craig is committed to spreading the good news in a bad news world.

—Kelly Wright
Host & Executive Producer
America's Hope

My endorsement of, "All the Green" is two-fold. I believe the true meaning of life that we all are searching for each, and every day will never be found without having faith, and this book brings that out! I've known Craig for over 12 years and working with him and witnessing his faith and the ability to bring out the faith in people, leads me to believe that Craig is not just a person who talks the talk — He walks the walk!

—Msgr. Jamie Gigantiello
Pastor Our Lady of Mt. Carmel Church
FDNY Chaplain
Host and Author of "Breaking Bread"

Title: All The Green: Discovering God's Plan for Your Life
Copyright © 2024 by: Craig Tubiolo

Published by: God's Plan Publishing
Address: 888 Holmdel Rd Holmdel N.J 07733
United States

Website: https://walkinfaithtv.com

Produced in conjunction with Goodwill Media Services, www.goodwillmedia.com

Editorial: Rick Kern
Cover design and interior formatting by *Hannah Linder Designs*

All Rights reserved under International Copyright Law. No part of this book may be reproduced or transmitted in any form or by any means, electronic or mechanical—including photocopying, recording, or by any information storage and retrieval system—without permission in writing from the publisher.

Unless otherwise noted, all Scriptures are taken from taken from The Holy Bible, English Standard Version. ESV® Text Edition: 2016. Copyright © 2001 by Crossway Bibles, a publishing ministry of Good News Publishers.

Scripture quotations marked NKJV are taken from THE HOLY BIBLE, New King James Version®, copyright © 1982 by Thomas Nelson. Used by permission. All rights reserved.

Scripture quotations marked NIV, are taken from THE HOLY BIBLE, NEW INTERNATIONAL VERSION®, NIV® Copyright © 1973, 1978, 1984, 2011 by Biblica, Inc.® Used by permission. All rights reserved worldwide.

ISBN Hardcover: 979-8-9867029-4-0
ISBN Paperback: 979-8-9867029-2-6
ISBN eBook: 979-8-9867029-3-3

DEDICATION

I dedicate this book to my father, Salvatore, or as we called him, Sonny Tubiolo, who is now looking down on us from heaven. My father profoundly impacted numerous lives, leaving behind a godly legacy that still resonates with me and everyone he encountered.

I know my father is proud of me because not a day passed when he didn't tell me how proud he was and how much he cared about me. Thank you for everything you have done and continue to do for our family. We love and miss you, Daddy.

CONTENTS

Foreword	ix
Introduction	xiii
1. God Gives All A Gift	1
2. Identifying Your Purpose	17
3. Distinguishing God's Voice from the Others?	33
4. Confronting Fear and Adversity	59
5. Leaving a Godly Legacy	77
Epilogue	97
Photos	101
Acknowledgments	115

FOREWORD

Anyone who knows me knows that I place tremendous significance on reshaping our lives and investing wholeheartedly in not just looking our best but being our best! And while focused routines such as healthy skin care, eating foods that work for us, appropriate exercise regiments, and similar life-dynamics are critical to personal wholeness, there's one thing that is easy to overlook—nourishing our heart and soul.

Just as Jesus told us to dig down to rock and build our houses to withstand life's storms, (Matthew 7:24-25), any architect will assure you that one of the most important parts of any structure is its foundation. My treasured friend Craig Tubiolo has crafted an outstanding book to help us begin within and develop an enduring foundation to build the rest of our lives on. Titled, "All the Green: Discovering God's Plan for Your Life," Craig walks us through the fundamental building blocks of a meaningful relationship with God and shows us how deepen our connection with Him.

Just as we learn to listen to our bodies and respond to them with nourishing practices, "All the Green" explains how to listen to the cry of our soul and shows us how to understand the heartbeat of heaven for our lives—that we might respond to God's love. Many times, we look at our faith unrealistically, and mistakenly relate our relationship with God exclusively with what happens in the four walls of a church. Craig clearly shows us that even though God wants us to worship together in church, He has given us all unique gifts, purposes, and callings. And that through these, He wants us to walk with Him, as our Master learning and following His masterplan for our lives.

While Craig is typically known for insightful and engaging interviews that draw deeply from the hearts and lives of celebrities, in a way he has done the same with the Word of God in "All the Green." His unique, everyday style has shined God's loving light and reality through the decorative stained-glass images that often obscure our faith because we don't understand God as He is, apart from religious accessories. While this may not be an interview with our Lord, Craig has been able to succinctly express the heart and life of God and describe what it means to walk with Him as everyday people.

He has tackled the basics and leaves us with a clearer understanding of how to recognize God's voice, overcome fear, and build a lasting foundation in a world that desperately needs Jesus. His counsel, wholly based upon the Word of God page after page, guides us in leaving a godly legacy through a life well-lived in deep and meaningful relationship with God—both in and out of church! You can't help but close the cover knowing that there is no better way to nourish our heart and soul than to draw near to and walk in true fellowship with the One who made them.

Ali Landry
Actress, Host, and Author of "RESHAPE your Life"

INTRODUCTION

Thank you for taking the time to read this introduction. I will value your time and give you a quick insight into what lies ahead in, "All the Green: Discovering God's Plan for your life.

First, I would like to introduce myself and tell you a little about who I am and why I wrote this book. My name is Craig Tubiolo, and some people know me as Craig Syracusa; I use the last name Syracusa whenever I'm working on any film projects or when I host my TV show "Walk in Faith."

I grew up in a low middle-class Italian neighborhood called Bensonhurst, which is in the Borough of Brooklyn, NY. As a kid, I always wanted to be in the entertainment business and had a passion for filmmaking; that passion developed into a career for over 25 years. And like most kids growing up in Bensonhurst, we were raised Catholic and attended church quite often; there was no negotiating in the Tubiolo household. My mother was strict, "No church, no go outside—no exceptions."

Even though my mother instilled this foundation of faith, I still lacked a personal relationship with Jesus Christ, but as a kid, I didn't think much about it. As I grew older and began establishing myself in my career, my faith took a back seat to focus more on myself and my aspirations of being famous and rich. On the road to fame, we tend to justify our actions and can become distracted by our selfish desires.

Over time, I grew lost, depressed, unfulfilled, and further away from my faith than I had ever been. Still, through a life-changing experience in Fatima, while filming a documentary, I experienced an "awakening" that changed the trajectory of my life, career, and family all because of God's love, power, and the grace He has for all of us. That experience was an opportunity for me to reset my life and my priorities and place my focus on God's Kingdom and not my selfish desires. I wish I could say it was easy or happened overnight, but it didn't, and I'm glad—it was a journey to self-discovery and transformation.

The flame ignited that night in Fatima continues to burn in every aspect, and now all I want to do is share my experience and the experiences of others with as many people as possible. My story is not unique; you will hear from some celebrities who will also share their story and how their life completely changed through the power of the Holy Spirit and a personal relationship with Jesus Christ. That encounter set them on a new path like me, who was once lost and unfulfilled.

As a host, I have interviewed hundreds of people, from celebrities like Martin Sheen and Jim Caviezel to CEOs, politicians, and athletes. The knowledge and insight that they used to accomplish and discover God's plan for their life are all in this book, along with the essential principles that are found in the Bible.

I constantly reflect on why God continues to use me as a vessel and why I'm blessed with having the opportunity to meet and share with some of the world's most famous and influential people of our time. I realized it's because I'm called to be a communicator for Christ, and whatever knowledge I receive, I know it's my responsibility to share with all of God's people.

I have found a common thread in all of the people I have met and spoken to, regardless of how rich or famous they were; without the principles of Jesus Christ, there was something missing in their lives, and when they surrendered their lives to Jesus, doors opened, and opportunities presented themselves. I share my journey, and I can also attest to that, for I have seen it countless times. But I don't want to mislead you into thinking this book will make you rich or that if you pray to God, you career will be transformed because this is not that type of book. Instead, this book is an honest account of what I have witnessed and what I have learned through all of the people that I have met and interviewed, but to experience what is in this book, you must be willing to go beneath the surface of your life and to be honest and ready to make some profound changes. I have plenty of resources and questions in each chapter to help you along the way.

Please feel free to contact me with any questions or if you need some guidance. I pray that at the end of this book, you will have a clearer understanding of God's plan for your life, how to discover your gift, overcome fear, the importance of leaving a godly legacy, and the principles of Jesus Christ.

You don't have to be a believer or a follower of Jesus Christ to enjoy this book and learn the principles I have laid out for you. This book is for everyone, and unlike many of the motivational or inspirational books I have read and researched, everything you need to experience a transformation and live a blessed life is in this one book. Please take a chance and spend some time reading and reflecting on it; I put my heart and soul into this book, and all I want in return is to reach another person with the message and information that was revealed to me.

May God Bless you and our time together
—Craig Tubiolo

CHAPTER ONE

GOD GIVES ALL A GIFT

Gift: noun
1: a special ability: talent
2: something given: present

Gift: (gifted; gifting; gifts) transitive verb
1: To endow with some power, quality, or attribute
She's been gifted with a beautiful voice.[1]

We all ponder the same fundamental inquiries: Why are we here? Where did we originate from? What is our purpose? And where are we headed? Though it may not always be comfortable to acknowledge, we're all on a quest for answers, seeking to grasp the essence of life. Like countless others, I too grapple with these questions about my existence, purpose, and destiny—where exactly am I headed?

We often like to convince ourselves that we are vastly distinct from our neighbors due to our external appearances. However, beneath the surface, we all bear the imprint of a divine presence, and we all harbor our own inquiries. I, for one, relish the pursuit of these inquiries. Perhaps that's why I initiated a talk show, "Walk in Faith," allowing me the privilege of addressing the questions that resonate within us all.

The inspiration for "Walk in Faith" took root more than 15 years ago—a divine seed planted by God during the early days of my career at Entertainment Tonight. If you're unfamiliar with the show I'm referring to, "Walk in Faith," let me provide you with a brief introduction to its background. The genesis of this show traces back many years when I served as a production assistant at Entertainment Tonight. At the time, I had just completed an advanced directing program at New York University Continuing Education and was eager to advance my career in filmmaking. Through a contact provided by a camera operator, I secured a freelance opportunity. When I arrived on the first day, I assumed I would be hired as a director or assistant director, but to my surprise, I was assigned the role of a production assistant (P.A.). Rather than letting disappointment cloud my experience, I embraced the opportunity with unwavering dedication. This experience swiftly humbled my ego and imparted invaluable life lessons that continue to shape my current career and existence.

What I cherished most during this period was the downtime I had, as I wasn't the director. This afforded me the chance to observe and listen to the host, Lara Spencer, and her interactions with the celebrities she interviewed daily. During my time at Entertainment Tonight, I had the privilege of meeting many remarkable people, and the memories of the experiences and events that I attended continue to be profoundly imprinted on my heart.

It was only later that I realized these encounters weren't about the events or the celebrities themselves; rather, they were about acquiring knowledge and allowing God to sow the seed that I've been nurturing for all these years. I never had the opportunity to express my gratitude to Lara Spencer for her inadvertent role in this, but I'm thankful for the time we shared.

Returning to the inception of "Walk in Faith," the seed I often reference began as a simple question: *Why aren't we asking celebrities more uplifting, spiritual, or positive questions?* This question simmered in my mind for years, eventually evolving into a desire to seek answers. This inspiration led to the creation of the show "Walk in Faith," where I aimed to interview not just celebrities but also athletes, CEOs, and anyone in the limelight, delving into the person behind the glamour and the lights. My experience at Entertainment Tonight had shown me a captivating side to these individuals, one that I yearned to explore, rather than the one presented with preplanned questions.

It's intriguing how many people inquire about the true nature of celebrities: Are they kind or rude? What are they genuinely like? My experience has shown me that this fascination stems from our desire to relate to them in a way that resonates with our own lives and struggles. Since most celebrities don't often share their personal stories, we tend to perceive them solely through their public personas. My aim was to transcend that superficial perception.

I've always been more interested in understanding the impact my guests hope to make, their emotional preparations, and the challenges they've faced, rather than focusing solely on their current film or project. I don't view my role as merely that of a host, armed with preapproved questions and nodding as guests recite rehearsed answers. Instead, I see myself as a communicator for Christ, aiming to inspire, uplift, and influence the audience through my guests, whether they are celebrities or not. I consider myself a vessel entrusted with a message meant for my audience.

I often tell my guests that I'm not here to fabricate a story but to narrate one. While I may not have fully uncovered the extent of my gift, I know that God has blessed me with the ability to connect with almost anyone He places in front of me. This enables my guests to open up and trust me enough to share freely and honestly about their lives, careers, struggles, and their faith journeys.

Through their stories, we have the power to inspire, influence, and evangelize those who are watching.

My gift lies in my capacity to connect with my guests, to be open, vulnerable, and attuned to their narratives and this openness encourages them to share more than they initially intended. I am, without a doubt, a communicator for Christ. My intentions and motives are never about self-glorification but about my guests and the potential impact of their stories on viewers. I am merely the vessel, and I am grateful that God continues to use me for His Kingdom. That's why I always say I'm not here to create a story but to share one.

People often seek the elusive "secret" or "shortcut." When someone does succeed, we may attribute it to them "knowing someone," which can serve as a way to rationalize our own limitations and validate our reluctance to act due to fear. Indeed, they did "know someone," and that someone is Jesus Christ. They understood the principles that Jesus laid out thousands of years ago, principles that are accessible to everyone, regardless of their faith, background, or financial status. Scripture serves as a roadmap to establishing a relationship with Christ. Along this journey, much like any other, there are exit signs, rest stops, and temptations to veer off course and bypass the great navigator.

Distractibility and discouragement can manifest for various reasons. After conducting hundreds of interviews, I've come to recognize a common thread among them all: the presence of a roadmap. At some juncture, each of them faced a crossroads. Some thought of quitting, some opted for shortcuts, while others persevered along their chosen path. What set them apart was their understanding of the plan; this knowledge empowered them to continue on the journey and ultimately reach their desired destination.

When we lack clarity about our purpose, calling, or God's plan for our life, including our ultimate destination, we often overlook the signs that guide us in the right direction. Consequently, many opportunities can become distractions or even lead us away from our intended path if they are not aligned with God's divine order. This can result in a life marked by confusion, disappointment, and unfulfillment.

My guests aren't inherently different from you and me, nor do they possess some extraordinary advantage, even though we might wish to think so. What sets my guests apart is their ability to recognize their purpose and to faithfully follow the path that God has laid out for them, regardless of external validation, the uncertain nature of the journey, or its duration. They place their trust in God's promises for their lives and have unwavering faith in His divine plan.

You must remain committed, and not be swayed by internal or external influences, discouraged by any circumstances or seasons. My hope and my intention in sharing this book are that, by its conclusion, you too will have the ability to discern your unique gifts and purpose. I pray that you will find the courage to step out in faith and embark on the journey toward the life that God has destined for you. I won't sugarcoat it—it may not be easy, but it is undeniably essential if you wish to fulfill your God-given mission and experience a truly fulfilled life.

I was raised in a loving Italian Catholic family in Bensonhurst, Brooklyn, by my parents, Phyllis and Sonny, an older sister, Michelle, and an older brother, Sean. Our household had a set of rules, and one was nonnegotiable: attending mass every Sunday and every holiday, without exception. The consequences were straightforward: "No mass, no go outside." When it came to my mother, there was no room for compromise or negotiation unless you wanted to encounter her infamous Sunday Sauce spoon. However, I eventually discovered that my asthma always seemed to flare up right before mass time; how convenient. Being the youngest in the family had its perks, as I was granted permission to skip church and stay home. It must have been God's grace because I was healed when they returned from mass. My mother quickly caught on to my tactics, and I found myself in the doctor's office receiving weekly shots to combat my "Sunday asthma attacks." I suppose you could say she won the battle.

My mother's deep faith was developed during her childhood by her mother, Mary. My grandmother was truly a saintly woman, a constant presence in the church, involved in religious education, and a dedicated volunteer. She served as my faith role model, consistently aligning her actions, words, and deeds with a life devoted to Christ and her family.

As I grew up, I didn't fully understand that both my mother and grandmother were persistently laying the groundwork for an unshakable foundation of faith. Looking back, I am extremely grateful for this invaluable gift. I often reflect on where I might be today if they hadn't taken the time to sow the seeds of faith in my life or if they hadn't considered it a priority. I can't imagine living a life without the solid foundation of faith in Jesus Christ.

It's widely known that organized religion in the United States has experienced a decline, particularly among younger generations. This decline isn't limited to Catholics and Christians; it affects all religions across the board. I've traveled extensively across the country, engaging with various religious leaders such as priests, pastors, bishops, deacons, and ministers. In all but a few of the places I've visited, it's evident that traditional religious practices are on the decline, while spirituality is on the upswing. You might wonder what exactly spirituality means to the younger generation. In essence, it signifies a personal relationship with a higher power, often shaped by an individual perspective. Many in this demographic do not align themselves with organized religion as a whole. Instead, they tend to pick and choose elements from diverse religions, science, philosophy, faith, doctrine, and even popular culture blending them together into a "spiritual smoothie." They combine these diverse beliefs to form their own spirituality, occasionally referring to their conception of God as "the universe." This approach allows them the flexibility to live life on their own terms with minimal accountability for their actions, habits, desires, quality of character, and sin. They can also adapt their belief system in response to changing societal standards.

Over the course of more than a decade, I've worked within the Catholic Church and other various religious institutions, and during this time, I've witnessed colleagues, friends, and even family members drift away from organized religion, each for their own reasons. Some argue that the church is out of touch and the Bible needs to adapt to modern times, while others simply don't perceive any personal benefit, making it a lower priority in their lives. It's often the case that when a solid foundation of faith is not instilled and nurtured during one's formative years, they are more likely to disconnect from the church or disassociate from their religious beliefs as they reach adolescence. I often wonder if more parents enforced the same commitment to attending mass as my own mother did during my childhood, perhaps we would witness an increase in attendance and a reduced decline in religious participation.

By the age of thirteen, there is an increase in young adults leaving the church, especially in the Catholic faith, it's around this age that they are preparing to receive the Sacrament of Confirmation. Confirmation is a significant and sacred event within the Catholic Church, marking the moment when a baptized person is "sealed with the gift of the Holy Spirit" and strengthened for service to the body of Christ. While some parents approach this with genuine enthusiasm and deep spiritual significance, others may merely participate out of tradition or for social media photo opportunities, aiming to please their relatives. It becomes challenging for children to perceive the value in sacraments or religion when they witness their parents' declining commitment to religious practice. This sets in motion a cycle. If this spiritually inclined generation lacks a solid foundation of faith in Jesus Christ, how can organized religion and the church endure?

However, I remain hopeful for this new generation of spiritual millennials and Gen Z. Both generations share a belief in something greater than themselves, an understanding of commitment, the ability to see past differences of race, gender, or status, and a commitment to a life of service. They seek a purpose beyond financial gain, and, most significantly, they embrace the virtue of love.

This lifestyle closely resembles the principles set forth by Jesus Christ. The only component they may lack is a foundation of faith, or more crucially, a comprehension of the profound relationship that Jesus Christ desires to establish with us. This is why I firmly believe that hope still exists. If we can instill in them the significance of a relationship with Jesus Christ as an essential part of their spirituality, we can begin a conversation that may eventually lead to their spiritual transformation. While some may view this as wishful thinking, as long as the fire within me continues to burn and there is an ongoing exodus from religion, I will persist in utilizing my gifts and hopefully inspire people to embrace a meaningful relationship with Jesus Christ.

Each of us are made in the image and likeness of God, bestowed with a distinct and specific gift. As the Apostle Paul assures us in 1 Corinthians 7:7, "I wish that all were as I myself am. But each has his own gift from God, one of one kind and one of another." Thus, it is our obligation to identify this gift and nurture it, enabling us to fulfill His divine purpose. A gift refers to something given willingly, without any need for payment—an innate ability or talent. Everything in God's creation serves a purpose; from the bumblebee that pollinates flowers to the tree providing shade in summer and beauty in winter. Nothing within God's creation is a mere accident; everything is part of a harmonious system, working collectively to serve a grander purpose meticulously designed by God.

While everything in existence plays a role in a greater system and serves a purpose, that purpose isn't always readily apparent to us. Numerous distractions and influences can cloud our perspective, including societal pressures, false teachings, the impact of social media, the opinions of friends and family, our own insecurities, selfish desires, deceit, sin, motivation, and even the allure of entertainment like Netflix.

Living in today's world can be extraordinarily challenging, as we are constantly bombarded with a barrage of information, diverse opinions, and an overwhelming array of choices. This inundation can leave us feeling confused, and rightly so. However, when we possess a strong foundation of faith, maintain a relationship with Jesus Christ, and comprehend the knowledge found in Scripture, we become better equipped to make decisions that align with God's truth, rather than merely following what may seem appealing in the moment or conforming to popular trends.

The Bible unequivocally emphasizes that each of us possesses a unique gift from God, and it urges us not to neglect or misuse this gift. This is corroborated in a number of passages such as, 1 Peter 4:10 for example, "As each has received a gift, use it to serve one another, as good stewards of God's varied grace." Your gift could manifest in various forms, whether it's athletic prowess, musical talent, or a particular aptitude for performance. The scope of potential gifts is boundless; it might encompass communication, organizational skills, teaching, mentoring, acts of service, or even the roles of a parent or caregiver. Your gift knows no bounds.

While many individuals may recognize their innate talents and abilities, it's essential to be cautious when others identify your potential. Ensure that their intentions align with your natural gifts and aren't driven by their own dreams or personal agendas. Regrettably, it's not uncommon for parents or family members to inadvertently impose their unfulfilled aspirations onto their children.

If someone perceives something in you that doesn't quite align with your natural gift, respond with grace, and then take the time to discern or pray about it before pursuing any particular path. As you nurture and develop your gift, others will begin to recognize and affirm your talents. Remember that God is involved throughout this process; nothing is purely coincidental, and events don't just unfold by chance. Think of it as God's way of guiding you along the right path or as a subtle sign.

Identifying your unique gift can indeed pose a challenge. If you're struggling in this endeavor, consider delving into your passions and then question why they resonate with you. The true answer may lie beneath the surface, and not be immediately apparent, so it's vital to allow God to unveil the deeper truth.

> I don't believe in coincidence, it's just God's way of winking.

Once you receive that revelation, take a moment to contemplate this question: *Is the source of this passion rooted in selfish desires, driven by a need to satisfy insecurities, accumulate wealth, or elevate one's status?* If this is the case, it might be worth continuing your search. Your gift should not primarily aim at amassing wealth, seeking fame, or pursuing personal pleasure. Rather, if your passion is driven by a sincere desire to serve, make a positive impact, change the world, support your family, nurture a child, inspire others, bring glory to God, or save lives—then you're indeed on the right path.

One common mistake people often make when trying to identify or uncover their unique gift is comparing themselves to others. It's essential to remember that we are all created in God's image but are inherently distinct. God crafted each of us individually, breaking the mold when He made us. We possess different talents, appearances, characteristics, experiences, genes, and starting points. It's our uniqueness that sets us apart and grants us an advantage. If we were all endowed with the same gift, appearance, and style, the world would be a rather monotonous place. Engaging in such comparisons can lead to feelings of inferiority, self-doubt, and fear—particularly if you are pursuing a path that requires putting yourself out there, being vulnerable, and subjecting yourself to judgment or even ridicule. Trust me, I understand this firsthand.

Understand that God created you precisely as you are, equipped with everything necessary to fulfill your purpose. Your job is to recognize your gift and diligently develop it until the appointed time arrives. This journey demands patience, which can be challenging, especially if you grew up in a generation accustomed to instant gratification.

> Don't wait until the rain starts to build your Ark

One of my favorite Scriptures that I've encountered numerous times, and which can only be attributed as the hand of God, is found in Proverbs 18:16: " A man's *gift makes room for him and* brings him before the great" (italics mine). I could dedicate an entire book to the countless instances where my gift led me into situations that neither my education nor my connections could solely take credit for. While some might argue that these are mere coincidences, you'll frequently hear me reiterate that there are no coincidences— only moments ordained by God. Here's just one example of how my gift and God's plan converged to bring this Scripture to life in my own journey.

I was invited to interview the lead actor of the film, "Palau the Movie," Gaston Pauls, a renowned actor, and producer from Argentina. Although Gaston and I had never crossed paths before, I felt an overwhelming sense of excitement about meeting him and delving into his faith journey, as well as his motivations for taking on the role of Luis Palau. Watching the film and witnessing his performance deeply moved me. During the screening, I was pleasantly surprised to spot my dear friend Dan Roebuck sharing the screen with Gaston. At that moment, it became clear to me that this encounter was not a mere opportunity to meet Gaston; it was a moment orchestrated by God. I sensed that there was a divine purpose behind our meeting, and I was more than willing to follow my intuition.

Our meeting took place in lower Manhattan at a beautiful hotel restaurant in New York City. As soon as we sat down to talk, Gaston and I established an immediate connection, recognizing that this interview held a more profound meaning and purpose. A portion of the interview follows:

Craig: Gaston, it's a pleasure to meet you. I want to thank you for the opportunity. I don't believe in coincidences, so why did God give you this opportunity to play Luis Palau?

Gaston: I lived in darkness for a long time addicted to cocaine, and after three nights, one night, I lifted my head and for the first time in my life said, God, please help me because I can't find a way out of this, and God gave me that help. This movie is another step in my path. I always say thank you, God. God met me in a good place, and that's why I'm here.

Craig: Being an evangelist or preacher like Luis Palau is a difficult path to take. People don't always agree with God or want to have anything to do with faith, and he was able to overcome adversity. Do you think if God called you to do something like Luis and be a preacher or to use your gifts to tell his story or share his message, would you do it? Would you answer that call?

Gaston: Yes, I believe that; I think God is always talking to us in this particular moment, and now I choose to hear and listen to that voice. Sixteen years ago, I was on my way to doing my things my own way. In the film, there is a scene where Luis is putting together a festival, and he says this is not for me but for the glory of God, and I believe that now. In the little things we do, even in interviews like this, we should glorify God and we can do that. It's not difficult.

Craig: Is there anyone that inspires you that you had the chance to meet, that changed your life?

Gaston: I met a lot of people who inspired me in some way, like Danny Roebuck., While I'm sitting here with you, I'm with the person I wanted to know. You have something to give me, and I have something to give you—energy, words, and feelings. I never thought about this before in my life, but now I want to know what God has for me in the next two minutes. I really appreciate this conversation. I really enjoyed it.

Craig: Gaston, you've mentioned a lot of adversity that you faced, and in the film, there is a scene where Luis has a breakdown, did you go through a similar situation with your addiction, and you knew there was nowhere else to turn except to God.

Gaston: Yes, while I was doing that scene I remembered God's voice and a lot of things about my life, my own life you know I told you that I've lived in darkness for so many years, so many years that when you see the light and when you start to pay attention to that voice I mean God's voice—everything changed you know, everything, everything changed and now I'm a different person. 12 years ago, I don't know who I was, but now I feel Christ here you know, God, God is here God is here, God is here, so I'm so happy for that it's my new life it's the real life this.

Craig: When your addicted to something or stuck within society's standards or cocaine, you lose sight of what really makes you happy and what's important and then when you're able to connect with God and your faith you see what the true meaning of happiness is of course.

Gaston: I thought maybe 12 years ago that a little powder you know it was cocaine and now I think, I believe that hell is there when we listen, we hear something about hell, hell maybe for me is just the size you know cocaine is hell. I mean cocaine is a lie and I don't want lies in my life now, I just need the truth, I need to live, to live in the truth and I need to believe that everyone in this world; everyone can find God and find the truth.

Craig: You're right and it's like you said, it's your mindset it's the way you see the world yes because you could see the world in a negative sense you could see the devil or the evil everywhere and you can also see it as everybody is love or see God.

Meeting and interviewing Gaston transcended the boundaries of a mere job or another episode. Through our interaction, we forged a genuine friendship, utilizing our respective gifts and conversations to inspire and spread the message of faith. Gaston's personal journey, marked by struggles with addiction and a self-centered life, serves as a powerful testimony. By sharing his story, much like Luis Palau, he has been able to lead people toward Christ. However, this all begins with the essential steps of identifying your own gift, discerning your calling, and aligning yourself with God's plan.

Take some time to reflect on this chapter and respond to a few questions as you prepare for the next phase of your journey, and perhaps you might want to watch the entire interview with Gaston, you can find it on my "Walk in Faith" YouTube channel. We have a substantial amount of work ahead of us, and it's time to embark on the path of discovering your unique purpose.

Reflection Questions

- *What are some of the gifts God has given you?*
- *What events or situations have you been exposed to that you know could only be the hand of God?*
- *Do you draw on these situations when fear and doubt creep in?*
- *What are you passionate about and why?*
- *When you think about what you are passionate about, how does it make you feel beneath the surface?*
- *Is your passion self-serving, or to hide something you're insecure about?*
- *What will your gift do to glorify God and point people to His Kingdom as well as make a difference in the world and your life?*

---

1. Merriam-Webster.com Dictionary, s.v. "gift," accessed January 10, 2024, https://www.merriam-webster.com/dictionary/gift. Accessed January 10, 2024

CHAPTER TWO

IDENTIFYING YOUR PURPOSE

You were born for such a time as this.
—*Esther 4:14*

Now that you have taken a moment for prayer and reflection on the previous chapter, I trust that the Holy Spirit is continuing to reveal the unique gift God has given you. It's crucial to recognize that you were born for a specific moment like this and designed to fulfill your purpose in accordance with God's divine plan, not your own. God did not give you a gift without designing a path, purpose, and mission for you to fulfill. Always bear in mind that God directs our journey and the probability of your birth occurring at this specific time is truly astronomical, numbering in the trillions. Much like the words Mordecai spoke to Esther, "You were born for such a time as this" (Esther 4:14).

This realization should instill within you a sense of confidence and hope, that you are not a mere accident, destined to aimlessly drift through life without a purpose. Rather, you are here to fulfill a distinct and divinely ordained purpose determined by our heavenly

Father. Your life is meant to feed your spirit, not just satisfy the desires of your flesh.

The word "purpose" refers to: the reason for which something is done or created, or for which it exists; and the word "exists" simply means to live. There are many verses in the Bible that reference the importance of living a purposeful life; so, the question I'd like to ask is this: *Are you merely existing in a world without experiencing the fullness of true living?*

> You were born for such a time as this.
> Esther 4:14

Given our understanding that God has a distinct purpose and mission for each of our lives, and recognizing that our days are limited, like a mist that briefly appears and then dissipates (see James 4:14), why do we persist in living in a way that falls short of the life for which we were created? For many of us, it often takes a significant reason or even a tragic event to begin the journey of self-discovery and change. Some wait until the start of a new year to make resolutions and embark on that path. It's important to acknowledge that transforming one's life is no easy task.

> Your life is meant to feed your spirit, not just satisfy the desires of your flesh.

As we approached the year 2020, there was an unmistakable air of excitement and optimism, considering it was dubbed "the year of clarity." Although I won't delve into the details of the trying times the world experienced during that period, many of us continue to grapple with the lingering effects of the pandemic. Nevertheless, amid the challenges, there was a sense of clarity that emerged.

Growing up, I often heard my parents tell stories of the "good old days," describing a simpler life. While I tried to envision what that era must have felt like, I could never fully immerse myself in that experience. They fondly reminisced about how the entire family would gather at the table to share meals and stories, bake cakes, reach out to extended family and friends on the phone to offer greetings, and spend quality time together at home as a closely-knit family, fully present and free from distractions. Their love for one another was unconditional.

But times have changed, and these are not the "good old days." And in our busy lives, it was often challenging to implement these cherished traditions, until the arrival of 2020—the "year of clarity." It was then that I finally grasped what it meant to live in those "good old days." This feeling wasn't unique to me; the entire world experienced a profound shift. We collectively understood the significance of pausing and being still. Not all of us had the means to bake cakes or reach out to loved ones, but we all possessed the time and capacity to reflect on what truly mattered and gave meaning to our lives. Consequently, we found ourselves pondering the question: *What is my true purpose?*

Perhaps it was contemplating our own mortality that inspired this feeling, or the rapid transformation of the world. For me personally, it took a pandemic to change my perspective. I wrote an article during that period, which was published, and I'd like to share it with you before we continue our journey:

HOW THE PANDEMIC CHANGED MY PERSPECTIVE

The dawn of a new normal is approaching, and I can no longer hide from the truth by remaining in my comfort zone or "sheltering in place." The world has changed, and I too have transformed; and I must adapt to this new reality.

I'm not talking about hoarding toilet paper or starting a chicken farm. Yes, those thoughts crossed my mind, my mindset and beliefs were rooted in a pre-pandemic world; and now we've transitioned into a post-pandemic era.

Many of us are so caught up in our busyness that we forget to pause and appreciate life. No matter how many times we see those charming wooden signs about cherishing moments over the fireplace, the message often eludes us.

Then time seemed to stand still, as if we were stuck in the movie Groundhog Day. However, it was far from the pleasant town in the film. It was confined within four walls, without the comfort food from the local diner. Suddenly, we had an abundance of time on our hands. They say time is priceless, something money can't buy, and yet we had more of it than we knew what to do with. We've all heard stories of elderly folks regretting how they squandered their time. But like curious children, we had to experience it ourselves, to touch the stove's flame and feel its heat.

Like most people, I was caught in a whirlwind of work, obligations, and responsibilities. I convinced myself that I was making sacrifices because I was working and supporting my family like a father should do and that my son would one day appreciate my efforts and that my wife should understand that I was doing it all for our family. I repeated these thoughts to myself while hearing my son cry as I left for yet another business trip or work function, or while saying goodnight over the phone instead of being there in person.

We often justify our actions by labeling them as sacrifices. However, it's a word we use too freely without truly examining our motives. Was I genuinely sacrificing, or was I sacrificing my family's happiness by missing out on crucial moments? It took a pandemic for me to realize that what I had considered sacrifices were, in fact, selfish pursuits based on my purpose and not God's. This pandemic unveiled many truths, from our own sin and mortality to our use of time, materialistic idols, relationships, lack of control, empathy, our foundation of faith, priorities, and our capacity for selfishness or love.

Some of us faced these revelations within the first few weeks. For me, God blessed me by revealing my sin immediately. I spent weeks reflecting and praying for God's guidance; and I guess it helped that I had the opportunity to interview dozens of people who were also affected by the pandemic.

One recurring question during these interviews revolved around the idea of returning to normalcy: would we retain the newfound clarity, wisdom, and appreciation for life, or would we slip back into old habits, confining God to the sidelines until the next crisis?

God isn't just a handy friend we call upon when moving furniture; He desires a daily relationship with us. I emphasize to others the importance of nurturing a daily relationship with Christ and discovering our purpose before we revert to the "new normal." We can't afford to regress into old, comfortable habits. I've undergone significant personal changes during this pandemic, realizing what truly matters and prioritizing my daily relationship with God. Without it, every aspect of life remains incomplete—a good marriage, parenting, and joy all hinge on this relationship. I need to demonstrate to my heavenly Father that I love Him and desire His presence in my daily life, not just during crises or on Sundays. I need Him every day. Through this relationship and His Word, I gain a deeper understanding of life. I once believed I had a relationship with Jesus because I attended church and prayed, but then I realized that I still didn't truly know Him.

I will forever be thankful to God for removing the veil that masked my own sin and selfishness; this awakening has drawn me closer to my faith, my family, and a clearer understanding of my life's purpose and deeper comprehension of joy and peace. God eagerly awaits our commitment to building a daily relationship with Him through Jesus Christ.

We're all on a journey; some are further along than others, while some are just beginning. My prayer is that you let God lead the way.

As we continue to transition into a post-pandemic world, it's essential to acknowledge that much has changed, including our thought patterns. There's a growing awareness that something vital is missing and identifying it can be a challenge because we've buried it deep within our souls. We recall sensing a subtle tug in our spirit as we begin our day, lie restlessly in bed, or sit in traffic on our way to a job that brings little joy but offers a paycheck. That uncomfortable feeling we continue to grapple with, and may have tried to ignore, is the sensation of not living in alignment with our true purpose and calling in life. Regardless of how much time passes or how busy we become, that sense of unfulfillment persists; it's God's way of nudging us.

Our lives unfold in distinct seasons, marked by times of sowing, growth, gathering, reaping, and reflection. It's safe to say that the pandemic ushered in a profound season of reflection. It compelled us to pause, turn inward, scrutinize our souls, and ponder the choices we've made and our future prospects.

> However, fear not, for that feeling has been reawakened.

Avoiding the pressing question, we all wrestle with became challenging: *What is my purpose in life?* For some, this period even led to questioning whether they had a purpose at all. The words of Saint Pope John Paul II, who once said, "We all search for the meaning of our lives," continue to resonate deeply with me. Indeed, we all seek our purpose and calling in life, and the season of stillness forced us to embark on this introspective journey.

Let me begin by emphasizing that it's entirely normal for us to question our life's purpose. Yes, each of us has a purpose; God did not create anything without a purpose. However, delving into the depths of our souls and examining the motivations and thoughts beneath the surface can be exceedingly uncomfortable. It reminds me of the old adage "sweep it under the rug." But there comes a point when you must lift that rug and uncover what lies beneath. That's where we need to venture. While it may be more convenient to operate and dwell on the surface, *we cannot step into the post-pandemic world with a pre-pandemic mindset.*

Many individuals lead unfulfilled lives, complete with regret and bitterness, even though they may appear content on the surface. Some shield themselves from the truth by filling their days with nonessential activities and tasks because, to them, busyness equates to progress. We often hear people proudly proclaim, "I'm hustling," as if it clarifies everything.

> But there comes a point when you must lift that rug and uncover what lies beneath.

We've convinced ourselves to take on additional responsibilities in order to project an image of success and productivity to a world where many others are also searching for meaning and significance. We have become preoccupied with creating the appearance of a productive and successful life, aligning ourselves with cultural trends and societal standards. Society reinforces this behavior by encouraging us to measure our lives against standards set by a culture fueled by consumerism and materialism. Society isn't concerned with our happiness or our quest to discover our true purpose; it operates with different motives. That's why it's crucial to shift our focus away from the hustle and recognize that we are being hustled by deception. We must cease comparing ourselves to worldly standards and refrain from obsessing over others as if social media is the gauge by which we measure our lives. These distractions pull us further away from our life's purpose, leading us to live lives that fall short of what we are called to be and truly deserve. Recognizing this deception can be challenging, especially for those who have grown up with social media and have placed their self-worth in the performance of their posts. This behavior fosters a predictable society, as we conform to what is popular and trendy, often losing sight of our own purpose while following the culture's dictates.

Many of us are consumed by various pursuits that neither hold importance nor bring us closer to discovering our purpose. I'm reminded of one of my favorite passages found in Luke's Gospel, where Jesus visits Martha's house; and Mary sits beside Jesus, attentively listening to his words, while Martha busily tends to many tasks. Martha eventually complains that Mary isn't helping, and Jesus' response is worth noting, "But the Lord answered her, "Martha, Martha, you are anxious and troubled about many things, but one thing is necessary. Mary has chosen the good portion, which will not be taken away from her." (Luke 10:41-42). Jesus emphasizes that we don't need to do everything; focusing on the right thing is what truly matters.

If you were to create a daily schedule detailing how your time is spent, you might discover that some of it is wasted on activities of little value, which could instead be directed toward working to fulfill your purpose. I remember reading a study conducted by Forbes magazine awhile back and though I cannot recall the exact issue it was in, I will never forget the data that the study unearthed—it continues to resonate through my heart and mind to this day... The study explained that over 900 million people worldwide feel unfulfilled in their daily lives, and some 70 percent of the U.S. workforce is dissatisfied with their current jobs. The study also suggests that discovering your purpose can potentially increase your lifespan—an interesting insight to consider.

> Jesus emphasizes that we don't need to do everything; focusing on the right thing is what truly matters.

Based on these statistics, it's likely that either you or someone you know is dissatisfied or unfulfilled in their current job or situation, primarily because they may not be living in alignment with their true purpose. Some individuals may choose not to pursue their purpose for various reasons, while others might still be in the process of discovering what that purpose is. What both groups have in common is a persistent sense that something vital is missing from their lives. Over time, this feeling of incompleteness can intensify and lead to an increased sense of emptiness and worthlessness, especially if we place our self-worth solely in our job rather than in God's purpose for our lives. It's essential to recognize that a job is temporary, whereas our purpose, which is our life's assignment, is enduring.

I'm not suggesting that you should abruptly quit your job or start a new business. Instead, I'm advocating for the application of the principles and promises found in the Bible to alleviate the stress and overwhelming sensation that arises from not living in accordance with your purpose. As believers, we are not immune to the feeling that we are not living up to God's best for our lives. God's promises and principles are applicable to everyone, regardless of their current situation, because we are all created in the image and likeness of God.

The Bible clearly states that God desires our success and prosperity, and it emphasizes that He is in control, not our workplace supervisor or even a pandemic. Jeremiah 29:11 assures us, "For I know the plans I have for you, declares the Lord, plans for welfare and not for evil, to give you a future and a hope." This passage alone should provide us with the strength and confidence to trust in God's purpose for our life and begin the pursuit of discovering and living out that purpose.

> This passage alone should provide us with the strength and confidence to trust in God's purpose for our life.

When you begin to uncover your purpose, life may not become easier, but it does become clearer and more focused. You no longer say yes to every opportunity or chase after opportunities because of the promise of advancement or financial gain. Just because an opportunity arises it doesn't necessarily mean it's from God or part of his plan—in fact, sometimes it's merely a distraction. In 1 John 4:1 the Apostle John says "Beloved, do not believe every spirit, but test the spirits to see whether they are from God, for many false prophets have gone out into the world."

What needs to occur is a shift in your focus and energy away from things that do not align with your purpose or goals. You might be wondering about activities like your fantasy football league, and while I won't address that specifically, I will say that certain things, including friendships, hobbies, and certain habits, may need to be reevaluated because living in alignment with your unique purpose according to God's plan often requires sacrifices.

Another common misconception related to discovering your purpose and having a relationship with Christ is that life becomes easy, and you will never experience fear, anxiety, or disappointment. Unfortunately, I have to dispel that notion. What it actually means is that when fear, anxiety, or disappointment arise, as they inevitably will, we are equipped with God's Word to better navigate these challenges before they overwhelm our thoughts and our spirit. Consider it like this: a negative thought is similar to a weed—it starts as a small seed that sprouts in our mind and if we don't address it immediately, it will continue to grow and dominate our mental garden like a tyrannical oppressor.

Throughout my career, I've been fortunate to interview a multitude of captivating individuals, ranging from Academy Award winners, to CEOs, to bishops, clergy, and everyday people like you and me. Reflecting on some of the most enlightening interviews I've conducted, I wish to impart the wisdom I've gathered in the hope that these words may also resonate with you and help guide you towards the path of discovering your purpose.

It's important to note that this journey may take longer than expected, as my grandmother often reminded me by quoting the old adage, "Rome wasn't built in a day." Interestingly, my guests, despite their diverse backgrounds and levels of fame, all shared a common thread—a deep, meaningful relationship with Jesus Christ. This relationship enabled them to identify their God-given gifts, align them with their purpose which was fueled by their passion, and develop the confidence to confront their fears. As a result, doors of opportunity began to open for them. In the book of Revelation 3:8 there is a powerful statement by the risen Lord that applies to the way their lives have unfolded. It says "I know your works. Behold, I have set before you an open door, which no one is able to shut."

I've witnessed the hand of God throughout my life and career, and while some might see these opportunities as mere coincidences, I hold a different belief. As a follower of Christ, I understand that God is in control, and shapes the destinies of men. Consequently, I perceive these moments as unequivocally God-ordained. My hope is that, by the end of this book, you might also shift your perspective and recognize God's hand in every opportunity, realizing it is not just happenstance.

One significant God-ordained moment was when I had the privilege to interview the authors of a book titled "The Impossible." This book later became the basis for the film "The Breakthrough." It narrates a modern-day miracle where a young man named John Smith fell through ice but was miraculously rescued and left the hospital without lasting injuries. If you haven't already read the book or seen the film, I strongly recommend it, as you can clearly witness the hand of God in this miraculous story.

Approximately two years after my initial interview with the book's authors, I found myself on a plane headed to Canada to visit the film set and interview the cast and crew. I had a strong sense that God was orchestrating this opportunity, and I was determined to follow His guidance. Once I arrived, I reconnected with the authors of "The Impossible," John, Joyce, and Pastor Jason, we spent time discussing the film's progress and how it all came together. I also spent time with the Executive Producer, DeVon Franklin, whose remarkable work and character have been a true inspiration to our faith.

What solidified this as a God-ordained moment for me, was that some three years earlier, I had interviewed DeVon Franklin and Dr. Oz in New York City about their segment "Faithful Fridays." Now, God had placed me in Canada to cover this modern-day miracle being produced by none other than DeVon Franklin.

Some may attribute it to a series of coincidences, but I firmly believe it was God working behind the scenes, for a God ordained moment.

When I'm granted the opportunity to conduct an interview, which I view as a true blessing, I approach it with the utmost seriousness and dedication. It may not be apparent to the audience, but I invest several days in extensive research and in preparing the questions for each interview. Furthermore, I am keenly aware that it is an honor and a privilege to use my gift of communication to share God's Word during my interviews. And it is important to point out that I regard each interview with the highest level of importance, regardless of the interviewee's level of fame or status.

Each interviewee whose spirit and achievements I explore, may curate their life in any number of ways. It might describe a sphere of influence or range of fame that splashes their status boldly across the headlines. On the other hand, it could leave their place in this world sequestered at the top of their resume as they pound the pavement. However, because God uses crooked sticks to draw straight lines and cannot be cornered, there is no telling what He will do with any given life. That being the case, fame, status, and achievement are secondary considerations as I dig into the buried treasure of a life and destiny—you just cannot know what the Lord with a heart that loves Him.

Zechariah 4:10 touches on this when is says, "Do not despise these small beginnings, for the LORD rejoices to see the work begin." For my part, I approach it all in accordance with Colossians 3:23, "Whatever you do, work heartily, as for the Lord and not for men."

While I take great pride in crafting my questions, I hold a fundamental principle close to heart: *I'm not there to create a story but rather tell one.* I acknowledge that, with the aid of my God-given gift and the Holy Spirit, a well-phrased question can produce a response that has the potential to influence someone's life. It might sow a seed of change or guide them toward Jesus Christ. If I can help just one person, then I consider my mission accomplished. I am, in essence, searching for the lost sheep.

I was thrilled that DeVon remembered me from The Dr. Oz Show, and I seized the opportunity to ask him about the importance of following God's plan for one's life rather than pursuing personal desires. This topic held particular significance for me, as I had once been that lost sheep I now sought to reach.

INTERVIEW WITH DEVON FRANKLIN:

Craig: You posted last week something about Chrissy Metz on Instagram, being prepared for this opportunity, how did you prepare for this opportunity?

DeVon: What I meant with that post is, first Chrissy Metz is one of the most inspirational people I know, so powerful, her story literally she went from obscurity to being known around the world, I love it because this is what God can do , we spend most of our lives being frustrated asking, "Well when is God going to show up" and God says get ready because when you go from obscurity to notoriety in 24 hours are you going to be ready, and what is so fascinating about Chrissy is before anyone knew her she was in acting class, she was doing her work she was going to auditions, she was putting in the time so when it came time to go she was ready, I talk about this all the time you have to be ready now, because the opportunity, it's going to be too late, for me in terms of preparation for this moment I spent, I've been in Hollywood for over 20 years, and I spent 18 of them preparing to one day make my own movies from starting as an intern to working as an assistant to a junior executive to an executive at a studio all of that was preparation years where I learned how to operate on set learned how look at a budget, learn how to look at a script, so this moment is a moment that I could not have succeeded at if I had not already being prepared for.

Craig: During those times or moments, when God hasn't necessarily answered your plans or prayers, sometimes it becomes discouraging, I know throughout your career, every time I see you your smiling, it has to be difficult, there has to be times when you questioned... How did you overcome those moments?

DeVon: I have discouragement all the time, even though things are happening I'm like God I want this to happen to, so the way that I do it is twofold I believe it's the Apostle Paul that says, "Forgetting those things that are behind and reaching forward to those things that are ahead...," so I forget and I strain, it's a continuous action going in both directions, at the same time. I do a similar thing, it's like instead of just forgetting about what has happened I try to remember that God allowed this and this to happen, so if He allowed this and this to happen then why would you doubt now that's not going to happen. I go back and look at my past—okay God! So, then that gives me hope and then I say what is the work that I need to do now to prepare, so I go back and think of the past to get hope and then I say what do I do now to prepare because every moment in frustration and every moment in discouragement is a moment not being spent in preparation so that is the tension. I manage to stay in that place of expectation and preparation so when things happen it will be a manifestation of what God already promised and I will be ready to meet the opportunity.

Craig: Do you think this story is all part of God's plan from John being adopted to John falling through the ice to John being healed to the book and now the film, is this all part of God's Plan?

DeVon: I think it's all part of God's Plan without a doubt and I also believe that God using the story to reach others is a part of his plan, one of the things that strikes me the deepest about the story is the adoption part, I'm not adopted I have adopted people in my family one of my nieces is adopted and we always had adopted people in my family and is so powerful for me. When your birth parents don't want you for whatever reason, you carry that with you so I do hope a movie like this and by John being so open and

IDENTIFYING YOUR PURPOSE

transparent and sharing his story with the world, that God is going to use it to bring healing to many people that are adopted and have a wound related to that, and a film like that might help resolve and heal it like that

Craig: Why did God pick you to tell this story?

DeVon: Man, I don't know, He said He would talk to a fool right, I don't know I try and be obedient and do what he's called me to do and why he chooses certain things, I don't know, when I get to heaven, I will ask Him and ask, why did You use me this way.

It was an extraordinary experience that continues to resonate with me. I remember calling my mother that night and sharing how I felt God's presence throughout the entire experience; it was a profound affirmation of my purpose. I've learned that when God plants a seed during a particular season, you must exercise patience, providing it with the necessary care, water, and nutrients for it to flourish and be harvested. Many individuals become disheartened and abandon their purpose before it fully comes to fruition because they attempt to gather the harvest during the wrong season, ultimately leading to a life guided by their own plans rather than God's.

When you seek God's guidance and place your trust in Him, you will have the ability to make thoughtful decisions, free from fear, emotional reactions, and impatience. My experiences, which are undeniably blessings from God, came about not through luck or connections but through His grace

> "Trust in the Lord with all your heart, And lean not on your own understanding; In all your ways acknowledge Him, And He shall direct your paths"
> Proverbs 3:5-6 (NKJV)

and love. I've come to understand my purpose and made the necessary adjustments to fulfill my assignment according to His plan. God's desire is for all of us to uncover our purpose. To achieve this, you must start by being honest with yourself, looking inward, and then making the necessary adjustments and commitments.

This is a question that many people grapple with: *How can I be sure if my gift and purpose are truly from God, and how do I allow God to guide and direct my steps?* In the upcoming chapter, I will illustrate how to "Discern God's Voice." This skill will prove invaluable as you embark on your journey of discovering your gift, purpose, and, ultimately, God's plan for your life. Once you've mastered this technique, don't hesitate to share it with others. Remember, life may not necessarily become easier, but it does become clearer. I would encourage everyone to make a resolute commitment to follow Proverbs 3:5-6, "Trust in the Lord with all your heart, And lean not on your own understanding; In all your ways acknowledge Him, And He shall direct your paths" (NKJV).

Remember, discovering your godly purpose is a continual process, and these questions are meant to guide your reflection and introspection. Take your time to reflect on these questions and allow God to reveal the answers in your spirit.

Reflection Questions

- *What brings me true joy and fulfillment?*
- *Why is it important for me to discover God's purpose for my life?*
- *How does discovering God's purpose for my life not only impact the Kingdom but also leave an impression on everyone I encounter?*
- *Have I been ignoring God's purpose for my life and living a life that was not ordained by God?*
- *When do I feel closest to God, and will living God's purpose for my life bring me closer or further away from God?*
- *Will living God's purpose bring me joy and fulfillment?*
- *What obstacles are preventing me from pursuing God's purpose for my life and moving in the direction where He is leading me?*

CHAPTER THREE

DISTINGUISHING GOD'S VOICE FROM THE OTHERS?

Dictionary.com defines Discernment as, "...the ability to recognize small details, accurately tell the difference between similar things, and make intelligent judgements by using such observations."[1] In Christianity, discernment can refer to, among other things, the process of discovering God's will in a given situation, understanding one's life's purpose, or distinguishing between the true nature of something, whether it is good or evil.

I hope this journey has brought you closer to identifying what you are passionate about and what your God-given gift is. I invite you to take a few moments of quiet reflection and revisit this question: *What is God calling me to do?* If you're still grappling with the answer, don't be discouraged; it took me quite a while to answer this question honestly.

Now that you've had some time to reflect on this question, I encourage you to jot down what has been revealed in your spirit regarding your purpose, even if you've never shared it before. Once you've finished writing, I want you to contemplate these questions and respond to them honestly on paper:

- How did that feel? Was it uncomfortable?
- Did you experience a sense of relief?
- Did you feel a sense of fear?

It's crucial that we understand that not every thought or desire we have is from God. Therefore, we need to evaluate what you've written down to determine whether it aligns with God's plan for your life or if it's driven by personal motives for self-benefit. This is the point at which we must be absolutely authentic with ourselves and delve deeper into the motivations behind our thoughts and actions. This is because it's quite simple to convince ourselves and others that we desire to lead a life of service or to bring glory to God when, in reality, our motivations are self-centered and have no genuine connection to God.

> "And when you pray, do not be like the hypocrites, for they love to pray standing in the synagogues and on the street corners to be seen by others."
> Matthew 6:5 NKJV

Accordingly, we must constantly conduct an internal audit, questioning whether our actions, thoughts, and motives are pure and sincerely aligned. I often find myself meditating on the words from Matthew 6:5, where Jesus addresses the issue of hypocrites, saying, "And when you pray, do not be like the hypocrites, for they love to pray standing in the synagogues and on the street corners to be seen by others" (NKJV). This passage prompts me to reflect whether or not I resemble the individuals Jesus cautioned us about? Are my intentions pure and authentic, or am I a hypocrite? The truth is known only to God and ourselves. While there are numerous ways to quiet our conscience and rationalize our actions, it's essential to be honest with ourselves and honestly examine our underlying motives.

While our times differ significantly from when the Bible was written, its teachings remain profoundly relevant, transcending culture and the passage of time. In our age, the advent of social media has significantly shaped our culture. In many ways, we've become dependent on these platforms, and some have inadvertently lost their true selves. The allure of "likes" and "followers" has led many to exaggerate or embellish the truth.

As you reflect on your purpose and God's plan for your life, I encourage you to remove the filters used for online approval and connection. Instead, strive to be authentic and honest with yourself, free from the constraints of seeking external validation whether online or from peers.

Have you ever encountered someone who said, "God spoke to me" or "God placed this on my heart" or "in my spirit?" The first time I heard this during one of my interviews, I found myself scanning the room looking for Jesus! While some might envision a scene similar to the burning bush in Moses' story, my experiences with God's messages have been more subtle. Rest assured, God has indeed spoken to you throughout your life; it's possible you didn't recognize or acknowledge it as His guidance. God is omnipresent, meaning He is everywhere, and He communicates with all of us. His method of communication is not typically characterized by a burning bush or vocal proclamations; instead, He has the most powerful form of communication; His written Word, the Bible.

Indeed, the Bible, for some of us, is the book that quietly rests on the table, gathering dust, giving the impression to friends and family that we're on a path to holiness; and I understand that the Bible can be overwhelming, but the good news is that it's not the only way God communicates with us. God can use a wide range of means, including Scripture, sermons, homilies, dreams, visions, biblical imagery, confirmation through others, prophets, hymns, worship songs, nature, books, thoughts, prayers, meditation, symbolic events, and even the beauty of the sun. We shouldn't try to limit the power of God or force God into human standards and constraints. Instead, we should keep an open mind when thinking about our lives and those moments when we've felt God's presence, protection, or received a sign that couldn't be easily explained.

It's possible that some of those moments when you felt a spiritual presence were God's way of communicating with you. Along my spiritual journey, I discovered that God was speaking and guiding me through various forms of communication like sermons, the Bible, books, prayer and meditation, music, and even my interviews. I have to admit that in my earlier stages of faith, I sometimes asked God for a sign or proof, which I've come to realize is not the right approach. God doesn't need to prove anything to me, especially not His love or His existence. His ultimate sacrifice on the cross and His resurrection should be more than sufficient evidence for all of us. I've been abundantly blessed throughout my life, and it's not because of my intelligence, charm, or connections; it's solely due to God's love, mercy, and grace. So, why should I ever doubt Him?

I'd like you to pause for a moment and reflect on all the instances when you believe God may have communicated with you or when you had a profoundly spiritual experience that defied any other explanation. We must also be mindful of 1 John 4:1 "Beloved, do not believe every spirit, but test the spirits to see whether they are from God."

This means that everything you hear, feel, sense, or see must be tested to confirm whether it originates from God. We should not readily believe every spirit; instead, we need to scrutinize and, as we would say today, verify. It's often simple to convince ourselves that something is meant to be or that it's a sign from God. It might indeed be divine, but we still need to verify and discern to ensure that what we are perceiving or experiencing truly comes from God and not from the enemy, our personal desires, or a self-serving agenda.

> Beloved, do not believe every spirit, but test the spirits to see whether they are from God.
> 1 John 4:1

Growing up, my mother rarely spoke about the enemy, who we

know as Satan. We understand from John 10:10, that Satan's intentions are to kill, steal, and destroy, and he possesses the ability to infiltrate our lives to try and do so. Furthermore, he is able to deceive us into believing that he has our best interests at heart while trying to divert our path by separating us from our heavenly Father.

Not every situation should be attributed to or blamed on the enemy. We need to understand that simply because we pray about something or believe it's a part of God's plan, it doesn't guarantee that it will come to pass. Blaming the enemy isn't always the answer; many situations result from our own choices, habits, lies, or self-sabotage, and we must live with the consequences. It's easy to lay the blame on the enemy when we can't secure a mortgage, while the actual reason might be a poor credit history due to our financial decisions. Similarly, we may attribute our health issues to the enemy, when in reality, we've been neglecting our well-being.

We mustn't grant the enemy power he doesn't actually have or invite him into our lives. Instead, we should take responsibility for our actions, whether good or bad. That's why it's essential to spend time in prayer and sharpen our discernment to comprehend God's plan for our lives. Doing so will bring a sense of peace and help us relinquish control, placing it in God's hands. This shift might be challenging for some, but it's crucial. Attempting to control every situation or casting blame rather than accepting responsibility will only lead to prolonged discouragement and bitterness.

> Consider Psalm 37:23, "The steps of a man are established by the Lord, when he delights in his way."

Consider Psalm 37:23, "The steps of a man are established by the Lord, when he delights in his way." It's liberating to know that God directs our steps, and all we have to do is be in a right relationship with Him. God desires to be involved in every aspect of our lives, not just in times of trouble or difficulty but every moment, every second. He wants to be there for births and deaths, when we need guidance, or simply a listening ear. God wants to be the first person we turn to when we have important news to share or for something as simple as looking for a parking spot.

We've substituted the love, guidance, and affirmation that only God can provide with "subscribers" and "followers" who don't truly understand us as God does. Instead of seeking God first, we've grown accustomed to asking for guidance on social media platforms or seeking advice from friends. A relationship with God is unlike social media, as it's not based on filters or personal status but rather on love, mercy, and grace, and it's accessible to everyone. That being said, rather than spending your days building a social media presence, invest your time and energy in developing a relationship with Jesus Christ, accepting Him not only as a friend but also as the way to your heavenly Father, and become His follower.

As you begin to develop and deepen this relationship through a daily routine of prayer, meditation, and discernment, you will begin to feel the presence of God, and you'll hear God as He begins to reveal and speak to your spirit. What God places in your spirit is what you must carefully discern. Take a moment to reflect on the passage found in Matthew 6:33, "But seek first the kingdom of God and his righteousness, and all these things will be added to you." This verse reminds us that being in a daily relationship with Jesus Christ is the most essential aspect of our lives, and it's through this relationship that we receive God's plan for our life.

We're all at different stages in our spiritual journeys, with some encountering Jesus Christ for the first time and others further along in their relationship. The good news is that Jesus meets us wherever we are. I wasn't always so deeply connected to my faith, and like many of us, there was a time when I prioritized society's standards over God's. I was more influenced by what was considered cool, trendy, or popular, rather than what was true and eternal. However, a spiritual awakening led me to reevaluate my life. I initiated significant changes in my life and towards my relationship with Jesus

Christ. I believe you, too, are ready for a transformation, ready to embrace God's promises over the empty promises of the world.

God continually seeks to communicate and guide all of us, however, to grasp His message, it's essential to listen with an open heart and learn how to discern His guidance. This process is achieved through the establishment of a relationship with Jesus Christ.

As with any significant relationship, you must invest time and effort to nurture it and foster a deeper connection. By nourishing this relationship through the study of God's Word, prayer, and meditation, your understanding of God's purpose for our lives will expand. Without a well-developed relationship and a comprehension of God's Word, it becomes challenging to discern His messages. Therefore, it's crucial to work on building a firm foundation of faith, as without it, we may overlook or misinterpret God's guidance.

Consider a common scenario we've all faced: the fear and apprehension that arise when we contemplate leaving our current job or career to start a business or seek new employment. Assume you feel dissatisfied or unfulfilled in your current job, but you are afraid to make a change because of your comfort and family responsibilities. This internal conflict is something we all experience—the fear of the unknown can often drown out the motivation in our spirit.

You may believe that God has communicated to you and confirmed in your spirit that it's time to explore new possibilities. But then you find yourself hammered by a chorus of loud voices, definitely not from God, undermining you with the dark disturbing assurance that it won't work out. These voices of discouragement suggest, "How can you succeed in this economy? You lack the education, no one in your family has ever owned a business, and you should just be content where you are." These are the lies of the enemy, aimed at diverting you from God's intended plan and purpose for your life. When faced with these challenges, and the voices pile on, turn to the wisdom found in 1 John 4:1, "Beloved, do not believe every spirit, but test the spirits to see whether they are from God, for many false prophets have gone out into the world."

Let me emphasize that the loud voice is not from God; it's the voice of the enemy. So, when you find yourself questioning that pure feeling in your spirit and doubt comes slithering in causing you to question whether you understood God or if He changed His mind because you're inundated by confusing scenarios—*remember* the Spirit of God leads, He never pushes! Maybe you even think that God is protecting you from future trouble, *remember* that these doubts are *not* God's way of warning you and He does not confuse His people.

These voices of fear and doubt may temporarily shroud the voice in your spirit with its purity, cloaking it in shadows. But again, *remember...* God is faithful and His leading is clearcut, so, if He wants to lead you somewhere specific, He will make His chosen path clear in time. And as He does, after a while, that positive and pure feeling will resurface in your spirit.

For the moment, you're in a state of confusion because you're receiving two conflicting messages. One is a soft voice, residing in your spirit, encouraging you to "trust and keep going," while the other voice is loud, often occupying your mind. It continues to insist that, "This will never work out, and you should stay where you are." In a state of confusion, we often turn to friends and family for guidance and advice, seeking validation for the answer we desire, which often aligns with the advice to stay where we are.

Now, let's use this opportunity to initiate the process of learning how to discern God's purpose for our lives and how to distinguish between God's voice and guidance and the influence of the Enemy. Take a moment to read and mediate each passage and reflection question before proceeding to the next step.

STEP 1:

Before seeking affirmation or confirmation from someone else, remember that God's voice is always consistent with His Word and aligns with Scripture.

Below are some passages to help you understand the heart of God as He speaks to us. May they help guide and strengthen you during this process:

> "For I know the plans I have for you," declares the LORD, "plans to prosper you and not to harm you, plans to give you hope and a future."
> *-Jeremiah 29:11 (NIV)*

> "For I am the Lord your God who takes hold of your right hand and says to you, Do not fear; I will help you."
> *-Isaiah 41:13 (NIV)*

> "Trust in the Lord with all your heart and lean not on your own understanding; in all your ways submit to him, and he will make your paths straight."
> *-Proverbs 3:5-6 (NIV)*

STEP 2:

God's voice is gentle and speaks to our hearts.

> "The LORD said, 'Go out and stand on the mountain in the presence of the LORD, for the LORD is about to pass by.' Then a great and powerful wind tore the mountains apart and shattered the rocks before the LORD, but the LORD was not in the wind. After the wind there was an earthquake, but the LORD was not in the earthquake."
> *- 1 Kings 19:11 (NIV)*

We understand that God's voice isn't restricted to just a gentle whisper, but if we hear His gentle voice, it aligns with Scripture, and doesn't contradict what He has previously told us, then we can confidently proceed to the next step.

STEP 3:

Draft a letter to God, expressing your questions and concerns. Afterward, write a response letter to yourself, imagining it's from God, and guided by the Holy Spirit.

This might seem a bit strange initially but regard and relate to it as a type of prayer. Similar to when we pray, it is a dialogue with our heavenly father where we communicate with Him, and He responds within our spirit. Don't worry about crafting a formal letter; treat it like a letter to a close, trustworthy friend. Personally, I envision a real friend before I start writing. This will be a personal letter to God, who is also your friend, as John 15:15 assures us, "No longer do I call you servants, for the servant does not know what his master is doing; but I have called you friends, for all that I have heard from my Father I have made known to you."

Thus, you are able to pour your heart out in your letter, addressing an issue, expressing a concern, and explaining the purpose behind why you're writing it. End your letter with the following sentence, "Dear God, please speak to me through Your Word and the Holy Spirit; write through my pen."

Here are some examples of questions you can ask within the conversation you're having in your letter:

- What would Jesus have me do?
- What is the Holy Spirit leading me to do?
- What choice or option aligns best with the biblical principles and Christian values I hold?

Take a few minutes to mediate on the questions that you asked within your first letter, then write a letter to yourself, now imagining it's from God, and addressing the questions you posed to Him. Allow the Holy Spirit to guide this process, and you may find God's message or answer being revealed. This exercise should all be done within the same timeframe. Make a determined effort not to get distracted with external activities and devices, find a quiet place and time where you can devote an hour to this step and begin writing.

If you are not comfortable writing a letter or feel like you would like to explore another method, I would recommend trying the *listening prayer*. I practice this approach regularly during the week, engaging in conversations with God throughout the day. It has been beneficial for me, so I urge you to invest the time and give *listening prayer* a chance.

STEP 4: THE *LISTENING PRAYER*

This is a loving, simple conversation with the Father, Son, and Holy Spirit. Learning the beautiful skill of the *listening prayer* allows one to communicate with God on a deeper, more personal level. By engaging in *listening prayer* with the Lord, we allow our relationship with Him to grow and develop into a two-way conversational friendship. There are a few steps within this exercise that are very similar to Step 3. You will need to find a quiet place away from all distractions where you can be alone with God and be sure to bring a pen and paper with you. According to the book of Ephesians, there are four voices that we typically hear while praying.

- God: The Father, Son, and Holy Spirit
- The World: Voices of others
- Ourselves: Meaning, our own internal thinking, desires, and rationalizations
- The Enemy: Satan

Before we can listen to God, it is important to distinguish and clarify what voice we are listening to, and how we address these other voices so we can clearly hear God's voice.

First, I would like for you to speak a personal prayer aloud to Jesus, seeking guidance or direction for something on your heart. Whether you're grappling with a challenge, seeking clarity, or needing assistance, express it openly and honestly in your prayer.

Second, I would like you to ask God a few questions. Here are some examples of questions to consider:

- Jesus, what are You doing in this situation?
- What would You like to show me or teach me about this?
- Lord, what are the next steps in this matter?

After deciding on the questions, you want to ask God, proceed to the next step, and bring them before Him in your prayer. Once you present your questions to God, take a moment to await His response in stillness and expectancy. Be attuned to what enters your thoughts, senses, and heart. In my experience, I perceive a small, quiet voice in my spirit. Write down everything you hear, sense, see, or feel immediately after concluding your prayer. Once you've finished writing everything down and believe you've received a message from God, test it by aligning it with the four voices. Ask yourself:

- Is this God?
- Is this the world/others?
- Is this my own internal thinking, desires, or rationalizations?
- Is this the enemy?

Once again let us mediate on 1 John 4:1, "Beloved, do not believe every spirit, but test the spirits to see whether they are from God..."

As you continue to mediate on John's epistle, I would also like for you to reflect on what you received during *listening prayer* and then ask yourself the following questions:

TEST IF IT IS GOD'S VOICE:

- Does what you sense align with Scripture? (God will never say anything to you that contradicts His holy written Word)
- Does what you sense align with God's character and His purposes?

TEST IF IT'S THE WORLD/OTHERS:

- Does it contradict God's Word and His character?
- Does this align with society or culture?
- Is this something you've heard or seen recently?

TEST IF IT'S YOURSELF:

- Does it contradict God's Word and His character?
- Is this your desire from a human level?
- Does it sound fearful, conflicting, condemning, or self-centered?

TEST IF IT'S THE ENEMY:

- Is it deceiving, condemning, judgmental, confusing, nagging, tormenting?

- Does it contradict God's Word and His character?

After identifying the voice you are listening to, set it aside if it's not God's. If it is God's voice, take some time to pray about it and ask the Holy Spirit to guide you in how to respond.

Sharing a glimpse behind the scenes, let me recount my experience with Stephen Baldwin. Despite being familiar with him and having mutual friends, this was our first meeting and collaboration. We arranged to meet at his upstate NY home, a few hours from our Brooklyn office. From the moment we arrived, Stephen and his wife warmly greeted us, creating an atmosphere that felt like we had been friends for decades. We spent over an hour speaking about his life and his journey of faith and then he gave us a tour of the property. I never saw a side of him that was not authentic or committed to his relationship with Jesus Christ.

People often ask me about celebrities' off-camera personalities, and I must emphasize that all the celebrities I've met have been kind and courteous to me and my crew, demonstrating their humanity beyond their public personas. It's essential to recognize that they, too, face challenges and may not always align with the characters they portray in the media. Understanding the pressures of the limelight helps us empathize with their experiences. So, the next time you encounter someone you admire, consider the complexity of their situation. And if you happen to meet Stephen or Mark, mentioning their "Walk in Faith" interviews might be a pleasant icebreaker. If you ever spot me, don't hesitate to come over, and say hello.

INTERVIEW WITH STEPHEN BALDWIN:

Craig: Stephen, have you always been involved in your faith?

Stephen: I've always been an extreme guy, it's why I drank too much and partied too much, I'm an adrenaline junkie and go fast and, you know, take chances and all that kind of stuff so for me the idea of extreme has always been a part of my DNA. So again, I was born into the Christian faith and it kind of didn't stick but then through a sequence of events when my wife and I were living in Arizona and I was doing a TV show for ABC when my first daughter was born. So, through my wife, who's from Brazil, we were able to hire like a nanny through family to come live with us in Arizona to help us around the house, be a housekeeper and help with the baby, cook food—it's in the Brazilian culture that's kind of a normal process. And this gal came to work for us, her name was Agusta, and when she came to work with us after a couple of weeks only speaking Portuguese to my wife, she explains, "Well the real reason I took this job was back in my church in a prayer meeting somebody said that God spoke and that if I came to work for you and your husband you would become born-again Christians and be involved in ministry in the future." So, my wife comes and explains this to me and at the time I was making more money than ever and just had my first baby and you know if this is my road to Damascus experience then you know life is good... So, after about a year of working with us, Agusta and my wife became very close and long story short, and over time everything Agusta said God said was going to happen it happened. My wife gets saved first, she becomes very intense in her commitment to her walk with following Jesus and in that first year of watching her that's the thing that really started to slowly work on me was I was already married for ten years to her at the time! This is fast-forwarding now; after Agusta we moved back to New York after the birth of my second child and that's when my wife got saved, there was that. Plus 9/11 and a sequence of events that kind of just made me have no place else to turn to ask the question what's going on why is all this happening why did my wife become born-again—like God what are you doing? That led to my making a decision, that I was now going to explore and investigate this experience but in a super hardcore way, cuz I don't know any other way to do it. So, I said God I said the prayer of salvation, I was baptized in water, I did all the stuff you're supposed to do, but then I made a covenant... That's a very powerful word if you know what its application means in Christianity. So, a covenant is you know till death do us part you know I did that with God I said basically if you'll show me your real I'll be Kirk Cameron on steroids I don't care what they say I don't care—if I know it's You, if I know it's real I'll go anywhere you want do whatever you want.

Craig: Stephen how did know you, you mentioned that He revealed Himself, can you share that with us?

Stephen: I'll give you an example. I'm Stephen Baldwin, I'm an actor, I'm this and that. I supported President Trump because as a Christian I believed that was the right thing to do. Cut to Alec Baldwin playing President Trump on SNL and the opposition that my brother and I have although we haven't spoken since the election because he's upset. But the very first Scripture I read that spoke to me supernaturally, was Matthew 10:34 which is in the words of Jesus—it says, "Do not think that I have come to bring peace to the earth. I have not come to bring peace, but a sword." What does that mean the sword is the division between those who will believe in him and follow him the way the Bible says and those who will believe in him and not do it the way the Bible says and then it goes on to say in Matthew 10:35-36, "For I have come to set a man against his father, and a daughter against her mother, and a daughter-in-law against her mother-in-law. And a person's enemies will be those of his own household." That's what the Bible says and that's a lot of everything that came out of my mouth in this world in the natural world with regular people. I realize how heavy that is and I say to those people how weird is it, but the first Scripture I ever read that like gave me a chill and this and that. It talked about if you love me first it may cause division in your family, and I haven't spoken to my brother since the election—that was 14 years ago. I read that Scripture and God, and He was preparing me then for what's happening now! Does that mean I choose God over my brother, yes, I choose God over my wife my kids because that's what I believe, that's what He's called me to. And what it says in the Bible which not everybody, like we were talking earlier, people pick and choose what they want to believe out of the Bible—so salacious...

Craig: 14 years ago, when you read that in the Scriptures, was that enough to sort of... let's say let's use the word "convince" you now or did you still have doubts?

Stephen: I went to a church couple years later and I'm listening to the pastor like this and in my head I hear, "You see that guy over there..." and I look and I see this guy with his wife and three little kids and one older daughter and I'm what I'm like, "Yeah thank you God, yeah I see the guy but I'm listening to the sermon so quit bothering me 45 minutes." In my head I hear God going, "When the service is done go tell that stranger over there these words, 'It's not your fault.'" For 45 minutes I go like this, "No I'm not doing that, that's weird I don't know the guy, he doesn't know me, what are you doing, why are you doing this?" I did. And then the Holy Spirit said to me "Remember when you said if you choose to follow me you'll go and do whatever I tell you to do when I tell you to do it?" "Yes, God I remember when I made that commitment to you." "Okay like I said go tell that guy it's not your fault." So, I go up after the service, I go up to this guy, I said, "Dude, I don't even know what this means, but it's not your fault. The guy falls to his knees! That day was the 15th anniversary of his first wife's death in an automobile with the 16-year-old daughter that survived, and this was his new wife and three new kids in that church on that day with the surviving 16-year-old daughter on the anniversary of the day his wife died in an automobile accident. Now brother, if that's coincidence to whomever, God bless you.

Craig: I don't believe in coincidences but there's got to be people out there right that sort of are praying for this; for these sort of signs, right, and usually during that period you're sort of burning the candle at both ends, right, you're like listening to God, but then you also, you know—do what you want to do, there must have been a point where you just broke down, right, and said you know "I need a sign," I mean did that happen to you at all?

Stephen: Oh yeah, the two examples I just gave you are two of 200 I wouldn't say there was one specific earth-shattering thing that I said, "Oh this is real," when I said to you that I read that Matthew 10:34, what happened was, I'm reading the Bible, and I felt a wind from the page has hit me in the face this thing is real this experience is whatever you, if it's Catholic if it's born-again, whatever it is... People need to understand you were born so that at some point in your adult life, when you know the difference between good and evil, sinning and choosing not to sin except when you have the knowledge of that. This experience is about simply; do you want to connect with God in the way that He intended so that you can live your life the way His will would have you?! Everybody's walking journey is different, I believe I'm called to evangelize in different unique ways.

Watching this interview again brought back so many memories and how grateful I am to Stephen and his wonderful family for opening their home and their hearts to not just me, but the entire world who can benefit from his impactful story of hope.

I'd like to share another impactful interview, this time with Mark Wahlberg. I was asked to interview Mark during his promotional tour for his new film "Father Stu," a powerful film that has inspired millions of people globally. Mark's films and his perseverance and outspoken faith in Jesus Christ have touched countless people and for me to have the opportunity to meet him was truly a blessing from God. As Proverbs 18:16 states, "A man's gift makes room for him and brings him before great men" (NKJV), and on that day, I was once again living out the essence of this passage.

DISTINGUISHING GOD'S VOICE FROM THE OTHERS?

INTERVIEW WITH MARK WAHLBERG:

Craig: Mark's it's a pleasure to sit down with you, when we discover God's purpose for our lives, we assume that life's going to be easy, and then the voice of the enemy comes, all the struggles, the storm, I can't imagine doing this film was easy, I can imagine you had to overcome adversity. Mark, how did you overcome the storm and what did you deal with during this six-year period making the film?

Mark: I mean it's never easy you know, it's not like I got a "no" from everybody I just kind of said to a couple people that I knew and trust that I thought might respond to the material they didn't and so I just figured you know the best way to do it is just kind of do it on my own. There's no interference, I have complete creative control, and when I make a film that I know is really special then, I'll bring it back to everybody and hopefully then I'll be able to get whether it will be the distribution that I wanted or the support of the archdiocese and everything else in between. I think it's just it's just a matter of staying the course it's hard to get a movie made—never mind, it's really difficult to make a good movie. And to be able to do both of those things with a movie that meant so much to me and is affecting so many people in such a positive and profound way, uh, well worth it, so um, you know no more, no more worrying about the difficulties of getting him in it's great.

Craig: I know it's difficult, like you said, you go through the storm and then you mentioned something that God puts people in our path for a reason but also too, God gives us opportunities.

Mark: And you need to be able to recognize it.

Craig: Yes, discern it, exactly. Why do you think God gave you this mission, there are so many filmmakers out there?

Mark: Because I've been spending 30-some-odd years; 40 years preparing to play this part in my own real life. And so, you know it's, why did He make me successful in film and television, the movies that He wants me to make are these kinds of films. I think He tolerates the other ones and maybe gets a kick out of some of them every once in a while, that made some good ones but this, God, it's so fulfilling to do something that has such a profound impact on people.

Craig: Mark, you know what I think it is that He can trust you because you're using that platform the right way because so many people are successful in the eyes of society and they have a platform; they misuse it.

Mark: Yeah, well how much talent is He willing to give you.

Craig: Right, exactly! He gave you the little and He trusted you with the big because you're using this platform, I mean like you said, your story, your life is very similar to Father Stu's right I mean there must have been a lot as you were preparing that you saw within yourself.

Mark: Yeah, Yeah and of course everything that I was going through even while we were making the movies, it's one thing to prepare to make the film and there's another thing actually shooting the film during principal photography, you know we're in the middle of Covid and I lost my mom it suffered many many many setbacks but you know I also got the comfort my faith gives me great comfort keep coping with things that I can't control.

Craig: Especially you lean on it, because even though being a believer, a follower of Christ, I made my sacraments in the church but there's still that time where I question especially when I'm doing things for my faith because it's easier if I'm just you know making a movie or a film it's still it's hard but it's easy in that sense but when you're stepping out in faith and you have a mission you know is to glorify God.

Mark: It's difficult yeah but it's also more fulfilling.

DISTINGUISHING GOD'S VOICE FROM THE OTHERS?

Craig: That's exactly right, it's fulfilling, you're not doing it just for money or for financial gain your brother Jim actually spoke about his defining moment, it was when Mother Teresa came to the prison, and Father Stu with the motorcycle accident and for me it was Fatima what was your defining moment when you finally said I'm going to surrender my life to Christ I'm going to really discern what he's called me to do?

Mark: Well I've had many but of course even getting into trouble at a very young age being a young kid who was completely lost and looking to all the wrong people for inspiration when all I was really getting introduced to was negativity and a quick quick downward spiral but when I turned to God there were many people there to support me and help me not the typical people we would look to not the kind of cool figures that represent the neighborhood and you know being a stand-up guy and all of those things but once I started focusing my faith good things started to happen for me and that felt really good I want to share that with people I wanted them to know what amazing comfort and joy I've gotten from my faith and share that with people and I think that will that will draw people like right to the faith yeah.

Craig: I agree—the one thing that I didn't know is according to His purpose so when I realized that it wasn't about me, I was an actor as a kid and I also got in trouble as a kid and I used to make deals with God and God if this happens right...

Mark: Yeah but it was in good times you know when I got down to express the gratitude I knew I knew where those good things were coming from you know I knew that at the at the root of it was all because of my faith and these rewards that I was given for doing good yeah that uh that's something I want to share with people I love it.

Craig: As we mature and get older and you mention it too, you know we want to do things that have real meaning like you don't just want to take a *job for financial gain how is this film sort of whether it's moved you in that direction or will you discern more has it changed you as a person.*

Mark: I'm talking about it now because I'm out here promoting a movie but I am not going to continue to talk about it in that I am sitting on a soap box and I expect people to acknowledge all the good things that I'm doing for other people and get a pat on the back you know as well as I do the left hand is not supposed to know what the right hand is doing and alms giving but in this particular time when encouraging people to pursue their faith to reconnect and all the things that this movie has to offer and the things that this movie will challenge people to do it will challenge them to you know figure out what their role in God's big picture is and how they can contribute even if that's lending a helping hand or saying a kind word to somebody that needs it but it's challenging people and challenging me just to do better and be better so that's uh—that's the mission that I'm on, to do good it's a reward.

Craig: It's a different feeling yeah, I know for me working in the secular world and then moving into the world of faith the reward that I get, the fulfilling, the sense of joy it's not just happiness that passes, its joy and like you said too, you have no personal agenda I mean obviously you want the film to succeed but I don't think anyone would ever say that you're on a soapbox or we see that there is a true meaning behind why you did this film yeah there was no agenda on here at all.

Mark: Yeah, I just look forward to also kind of being out there and just doing good work as opposed to just talking about it. I love it I love it, a lot of people do this and I get it this is a big part of the job but uh, you know going out there doing good work empowering other people to find their purpose and putting them in a position to be successful and expressing their abilities through their talents I mean that's something that I really look forward to.

Craig: I love it and even in the film too like for me it resonated that even a sinner... God will take any of us I mean look at you, you were broken.

Mark: He's looking for the broken more than anybody, exactly!

Craig: Yeah, I agree I think for me too he picked someone like me because I'm on fire for my faith now because of what I went through, and because I have that story that I can use same as you talk to people that might not open up a Bible but might watch a film.

Mark: But also, people that are going through something similar to what you've gone through and you have the experience and therefore the credibility and authenticity to speak about it because you've been through it and Father Stu was so effective in that way it was prison ministry. All the things that he did I mean he spoke the people's language you know he was one of them and they recognized that right away—people know the difference.

Craig: As my friend Art would say, "The street creds."

Mark Wahlberg: Exactly, thanks for all you do.

In closing this chapter, I want to acknowledge Bonnie Weiss, the founder and director of the "Center for Christian Coaching," for making this chapter possible through her teaching and guidance. To learn more about The Center for Christian Coaching and explore the opportunities of becoming a Christian life coach, please visit their website located at: www.centerforchristiancoaching.com.

You can also email her at support@centerforchristiancoaching.com and if you do, please let Bonnie know that I referred you.

Visit us on You Tube:
Walk In Faith Craig Syracusa
@walkinfaithcraigsyracusa4339
https://www.youtube.com/channel/UCh-AraNNi-8XAmj4M9jB8lg

I pray that these interviews have impacted you, and I advise you to log on to my YouTube page to watch the entire episode.

The next time you encounter a challenge or stand at a crossroad seeking guidance, you will be better equipped to discern which path to take and whose voice is guiding you along the journey. Before you move on to the next chapter consider taking some time to answer the following questions:

Reflection Questions:

- *In what ways does God communicate with you?*
- *Reflecting on your life, what discernments have you made?*
- *Are you at a level of spiritual maturity where you seek God's guidance before making decisions?*
- *Looking back, is there a decision you wish you had sought God's guidance on?*
- *How do you engage in communication with God?*
- *What are some channels through which God communicates with us?*

---

1. Dictionary.com. "discernment," accessed January 17, 2024, https://www.dictionary.com/browse/discernment

CHAPTER FOUR

CONFRONTING FEAR AND ADVERSITY

*For God has not given us a spirit of fear,
but of power and of love and of a sound mind.*
—2 Timothy 1:7 (NKJV)

This chapter holds immense significance in fulfilling God's plan for your life. To take the leap of faith, one must learn to identify, neutralize, and push through the fears that can dictate the course of the future. Yielding to fear can stop you from fulfilling your purpose, potentially leading to a life of regret. Fear, often subtle and elusive, may disguise itself as a protective instinct against harm. It manifests in various forms, and personally, it remains a challenge for me. Below, I've placed a well-known acronym that hits the nail on the head with respect to understanding the dynamics of fear:

False
Evidence
Appearing
Real

However, despite reading and reciting quotes, acronyms, and Bible passages, the struggle with fear persists. Often, there is no truth behind the fears I harbor. We can convince ourselves that the evidence presented in our thoughts is valid, but those thoughts can stem from insecurities, past experiences, lies of the enemy, a lack of trust and knowledge in God's Word, distractions, or simply allowing negative thoughts to take root in our spirit.

Acknowledging and identifying what causes fear doesn't always prevent its grip. The Bible provides clarity on fear, stating in 2 Timothy 1:7, "For God has not given us the spirit of fear; but of power, and of love, and of a sound mind" (NKJV). Reflecting on this verse, I realize I possess power and love, but perhaps my mind is not sound. Despite reading this passage numerous times, I still struggle with fear, which raises the question, what thoughts am I allowing to enter my spirit, leading to a state of fear or an unsound mind?

Fear can be defined as an emotional and physiological response to a perceived threat or danger. It is a natural, adaptive reaction that prepares the body to respond to situations that may pose harm. Fear triggers various physical and psychological changes, such as heightened alertness, increased heart rate, and a sense of unease. While fear is crucial for survival, excessive or irrational fear can lead to anxiety disorders and impact our overall well-being.

> Timothy 1:7, "For God has not given us the spirit of fear; but of power, and of love, and of a sound mind" (NKJV)

In our lives, it's evident that fear is a genuine emotional response that affects us all. We experience moments when we sense or detect fear, times when we conquer it by facing our fears, and times when fear paralyzes us. Personally, I fear heights and struggle with climbing ladders due to a fear of losing my balance and falling. I have never fallen off a ladder or witnessed anyone falling off a ladder but yet that emotional response limits what I can do. To confront this fear, I decided to go skydiving, and although I jumped out of a plane twice at 10,000 feet, I still struggle with climbing a ladder. Although the probability of falling off a ladder is slim, the fear persists. Fear takes many forms, and despite my fear of falling, I climb the ladder to decorate for Christmas because the goal outweighs the fear that grounds me.

Consider fear in the context of fulfilling God's plan and the adversity encountered, especially when aligning with God's purpose over personal agendas. It seems the enemy intensifies its efforts to instill fear when we pursue our purpose and is less active when we are not. Reflect on moments in your life when pursuing something for the Kingdom prompts fear, doubt, or negative thoughts. How often do we hear people reciting the quote from Oscar Wilde, "No good deed goes unpunished?" Perhaps we should reframe it to say, "It's only the God-deeds that the enemy comes to punish us for."

> Perhaps we should reframe it to say, "It's only the God-deeds that the enemy comes to punish us for."

I haven't always been so attuned to myself and God's Word, and although I have recited that quote in the past, I've never believed its words or allowed it to take root in my spirit. People often ask me about my unwavering commitment to my faith and my ongoing mission to evangelize and inspire people to cultivate a daily relationship with Jesus Christ. In the past, I could only share my story with a limited audience. Thanks to my show and the platform it provides, I can now share my testimony with anyone seeking it.

I strive to reach people like my former self — individuals searching for truth. I discovered this truth through the people I've met and interviewed. They all shared a commonality: *they applied the principles and promises of Jesus Christ.* My desire to share this knowledge and information with as many people as possible stems from my own past experiences. I was once lost, chasing my dreams and desires, negotiating with God as if I knew better than Him.

Reflecting on my younger days, I wish I had possessed this knowledge to guide me. However, the still, small voice of God reminds me that my personal experiences, learned through trials and tribulations, enable me to teach others more effectively.

Each chapter represents a milestone in my life, holding unique significance, and has impacted me in various ways. Writing this book feels like reliving each experience, and there have been moments during this process when I struggled in certain areas, especially when it comes to fear. In those times, I revisited my own words to remind myself of the glory of God, countering the ease with which self-doubt can creep in. The enemy is always ready to condemn and exploit our insecurities.

During this period, I underwent significant shifts in both my personal life and career. I lost my father, experienced a job change, and navigated through the challenges of the pandemic. These moments brought forth fear, doubt, and adversity, being a believer and follower of Christ doesn't make us immune to such feelings and experiences. Instead, it equips us with the means to respond in the way Jesus taught us.

> **The enemy is always ready to condemn and exploit our insecurities.**

As I sit here in the midst of another storm, I acknowledge that adversity, once overwhelming, now feels like a light breeze. However, the voice of the enemy occasionally attempts to anchor my soul to fear, doubt, and confusion. In those moments, I remind myself of powerful biblical truths found in passages such as Psalm 112:7, "He will not be afraid of evil tidings; His heart is steadfast, trusting in the Lord" (NKJV). And Isaiah 54:17, "'No weapon formed against you shall prosper, And every tongue which rises against you in judgment You shall condemn. This is the heritage of the servants of the Lord, And their righteousness is from Me,' Says the Lord" (NKJV). The journey of following Jesus is not always easy, but it is spiritually rewarding, offering a peace that transcends financial gains.

It's crucial to search beneath the surface of our thoughts and reasoning, asking God to reveal the truth. If there's a personal or secret agenda, God will bring these to light within our spirit, helping us understand the internal struggles and reasons behind our lack of peace.

Fear often distorts our motives, convincing us that we're following God's plan when, in reality, our intentions are rooted in increasing our status and financial stability. Honesty about what lies beneath the surface is essential, separating personal motives from a genuine calling from God.

For example, if God reveals that financial gain motivates us, it's essential not to worry excessively! These motives are most likely influenced by fear—a tactic used by the enemy that can lead to worry, doubt, anxiety, and depression. Identifying and controlling these thoughts is crucial to prevent them from taking root.

Fear frequently manifests as reminders of insecurities and past failures, urging us to give up. Recognizing these lies as the distractions they are is essential. God wouldn't bring us this far only to abandon us, and how could those thoughts be from God if we are made in His image.

Consistent reading and meditation on God's Word are vital to combat the enemy's lies and deception. Fear is not an attribute of God, and it's a battle we must continually face. For instance, I faced nightly panic episodes at 2 a.m., worrying about various aspects of life. Surrendering these concerns to God and speaking them out loud helped, but the thoughts returned. Recognizing the enemy's tactics, especially during vulnerable moments like sleep, is crucial. By consistently surrendering worries to God, we can prevent the enemy's attempts to control our minds and steal our peace. The Bible serves as our powerful weapon in this ongoing battle.

If you have noticed the repeated use of military-related language, there is a very practical reason for it. When we surrender our lives to Christ, the reality is that we are enrolled in a great conflict. Because of this, words like "combat," "tactics," "enemy," "battle, "and "weapon" appear in our speech as they describe the reality we have chosen to live out by default when we choose to live for Christ.

And because they are agents of the enemy, we need to address our fears and thoughts, and for me, vocalizing them and reciting Scripture consistently helps. When fear subsides, and peace settles in, it's crucial to scrutinize the thought, examining its root cause and origin. I live in New Jersey with plenty of grass and trees and I struggle with keeping up with the excessive weeds that seem to grow throughout the year. Fear is similar to a weed; it's seeds actively seek opportunities to sprout and grow searching for the opportunity to latch onto something and choke that which is godly so it can't continue to grow.

> **Like the weed preventer we must spray and pray on a daily basis**

Reading Scripture is similar to a weed preventer, you treat the soil by applying the preventer which builds a barrier to block and prevent the weed from taking root. The barrier might be invisible, but we put our trust in the manufacture, which assures us that its product will prevent the seed from taking root or growing. Similarly, Scripture and trusting in God's Word is how we can combat fear, because fear is the persistent weed seeking opportunities to take root in our spiritual garden and God's Word acts as the preventative measure applied to counteract the weed's growth.

Like the weed preventer we must spray and pray on a daily basis, creating a daily routine in order for our spiritual garden to flourish without weeds of fear taking root. Being in a daily relationship with Jesus and building a routine around prayer and meditation is the strongest way of preventing fear from taking root in your spirit. It's hard to possess a sound mind if you are not in His Word or speaking to God throughout the day. You might still wake up at 2 a.m. but those thoughts will not overwhelm you because you have built a barrier and a foundation of faith in His Word so the fear that attempts to creep in will be neutralized.

Growing up in the Catholic Church, it was not customary for the priest to openly discuss his personal fears or anxieties. I was under the impression that he must have everything in order, and due to his personal relationship with Jesus Christ, he was immune to fear and depression. Therefore, I decided to hide my own fears, anxieties, and depressions, fearing that sharing them might lead to being perceived as less than I should be.

During the pandemic, I had the opportunity to conduct numerous interviews per day from my home office and studio. I distinctly remember interviewing a priest who had battled the COVID virus, and I posed the question of whether he was afraid to die. His honest response was yes. While some might have expected a different answer, such as expressing anticipation of being with the heavenly Father or emphasizing the transient nature of life, his candid acknowledgment surprised me. I continue to reflect on that interview as it revealed that even a devoted follower of Christ, a priest, or a spiritual leader can grapple with fear. I didn't have a follow-up question, as I, too, fear death, primarily due to the thought of leaving my son and wife behind. And although I look forward to being reunited with my heavenly Father and loved ones in heaven, I still struggle in that area.

Could the spirit of fear have been inherited by all humans along with original sin? In Genesis 3:10, Adam acknowledges his fear and hides from God, stating, "I heard Your voice in the garden, and I was afraid because I was naked; and I hid myself" (NKJV). In Genesis 3:11, God says, "Who told you that you were naked?" While God doesn't explicitly mention Adam's fear, one may ponder whether the spirit of fear has been passed down to his descendants.

Similar to Adam's honesty with God about his fear, we too should be open and willing to express our fears to God. By being honest with God and ourselves and developing trust in Him, we can seek His guidance. Surrendering our fears to the Lord means relying on His strength rather than our own. When I verbalize to God that I surrender my fears, worries, hurts, anxieties, and depression, I experience a sense of relief and peace. Although it may return in different forms, my weed analogy holds true—fear continually seeks opportunities to grow.

I've come to understand that when you are aligned with God's plan, it's likely that you will face spiritual attacks rooted in fear, adversity, and ongoing struggles. The enemy tends to target those who are actively seeking to live according to God's best, fostering a relationship with Christ, and fulfilling His promises.

> Although it may return in different forms, my weed analogy holds true—fear continually seeks opportunities to grow.

If someone appears to go through life without encountering fear or adversity, it's essential to scrutinize their situation. More often than not, it indicates that the enemy has successfully placed them exactly where he wants them—separated from God and His intended purpose for their life.

In my extensive interviews with some of the most successful individuals, no one has ever described the journey as easy or free from challenges. Fear and adversity consistently accompany God's purpose and plan for one's life. When I encounter people with significant dreams or a passion for spreading the gospel, I reflect on my own life and its inherent challenges. We find ourselves contending with a culture and society reluctant to acknowledge the truth about Jesus Christ and our Christian faith. Expecting this path to be easy is unrealistic. This underscores the importance of being deeply rooted in Scripture, maintaining a daily relationship with Jesus, and sharing our personal journeys and testimonies to inspire and impact the next generation, preventing them from falling prey to the lies.

A study revealed that the only two fears we are born with are the fear of falling and the fear of loud noises. However, as we navigate through life, additional fears tend to develop. The question then arises, *How can we manage and control these fears, ensuring that they don't dictate our actions and that we can live beyond their constraints?*

Fear is a universal emotion, yet the specific things we fear can differ greatly among individuals. Life experiences, circumstances, trauma, family dynamics, insecurities, limited knowledge, and a lack of faith are among the various reasons that contribute to the development of fears throughout our lifetime. These fears have the potential to hinder us from leading a fulfilled life.

In order to uncover the root cause of your fears, you must engage in soul-searching and self-evaluation. Explore the origins of specific fears, which may have been influenced by your upbringing or environment. It's essential to identify and break the cycle of these fears to prevent them from transferring to future generations. To do so, I recommend dedicating time to meditation and prayer, reflecting on memories associated with when you first experienced or sensed fear. Be honest with yourself to recall these memories. One prevalent fear is the fear of change, particularly in relation to our jobs or the unknown.

Often, we prefer being in a familiar and controllable situation rather than to risk stepping out in faith and facing our fears. Having control over a situation doesn't necessarily mean the situation is a positive one, but it is familiar, and we would rather be in a familiar situation than a situation that we can't control.

In her youth, my wife experienced a traumatic event when she was hit by a car, leading to a long-standing fear of driving. Overcoming this fear required years of effort and self-examination. We delved into the root cause of her fear and devised strategies to overcome it.

For an extended period, she held the belief that she would never drive. However, circumstances changed when we moved to a remote area in New Jersey, where public transportation was not readily available. This shift forced her to confront the fear, which had been feeding off her dependence on public transportation. Overcoming this fear proved to be a transformative journey toward independence.

It's worth noting that not all fears are easily identifiable and overcoming them without addressing the root cause may lead to the emergence of a new, more challenging version of the fear. Our brains are wired to prioritize safety, prompting us to avoid situations that trigger fear or discomfort. This response is often rooted in self-preservation and survival instincts. However, it's important to recognize that these signals are not always grounded in factual information or a comprehensive understanding of the potential outcomes. Instead, they reflect our tendency to navigate the world based on the fears we've cultivated, maintaining a cycle of fear-driven decision-making.

Our brains will steer us away from situations that extend beyond our fears or comfort zones. This is where trust and faith in God become crucial. By placing your trust in God and having faith that you can overcome these feelings, reminding yourself that God is in control—not the fears that preside over you—you can start living a life that transcends fear.

We must also recognize that we can manage our emotions and feelings which brings a sense of ease to life. Trusting that God will not abandon us but instead empower and equip us to conquer feelings of fear should provide comfort. Some fears can be controlled through genuine faith in God and His plan, while others may be eradicated by stepping out in faith and disregarding the fear.

Having unwavering faith and trust in God's plan while still experiencing fear can be challenging. However, when we fully rely on God's Word and understand that He holds us in the palm of His hand, fear becomes less dominant compared to moments of doubt or when seeking external solutions.

When you begin to sense the emotion of fear, reflect on the instances when God helped you overcome the adversity and chal-

CONFRONTING FEAR AND ADVERSITY

lenges and meditate on those experiences, preventing the fear-seed from taking root. This is not a one-time practice; maintaining a daily relationship with Jesus Christ and His Word is crucial. Remember, you can choose to live God's plan for your life or live the enemy's.

> **Remember, you can choose to live God's plan for your life or live the enemy's.**

When contemplating fear and the voice of the enemy, my thoughts immediately turned to the numerous interviews I conducted with professional athletes and world champion boxers. Despite rigorous training, a level of fear accompanies them on the field and into the ring and I suggest you spend time watching the entire interviews on my channel.

After some time of reflection, I considered two distinct interviews where both individuals grappled with negative self-talk and fear and since they could not rely on athleticism, they utilized something more relatable, a spiritual daily routine to overcome these emotions.

Natasha Bure, the daughter of Candace Cameron Bure, offered her insights on a shared fear during her teenage years and strategies to overcome it in one interview. Another interview featured my friend Ali Landry, who authored an inspirational book chronicling her spiritual journey, describing how she triumphed over tragedies, and the emphasis on maintaining a daily routine.

To conquer fear, anxiety, and insecurities, building trust requires unwavering faith in Jesus Christ, His Word, and promises. Nurturing this relationship involves spending daily quality time with Him. Personally, when I deviate from my routine, I risk succumbing to insecurities, negative self-talk, and the insidious voice of the enemy attempting to sow fear. Ali emphasizes the significance of a daily routine while Natasha speaks about a personal fear. These insights from the interviews underscore that fear is universal, affecting all, even children.

We must actively combat negative self-talk and the encroaching fear. Regardless of age, gender, or status, we are all vulnerable to fear but the key to overcoming it lies in *establishing a daily routine*. As admirable or impressive as our achievements may be, the fact is that no matter how successful or wealthy one is, the enemy's voice can still find its way in. Through my experiences, I've learned that initiating each day with God's Word, meditation, or solitude is crucial, it's important to set the right tone for the day. Many individuals begin their day by checking their phones or watching the news, often leading to a morning filled with stress and anxiety. While there are many things beyond our control, we can choose to set a positive tone for our day by creating a daily spiritual routine.

Ali Landry's resume offers up an impressive serving of both depth and breadth. Crowned Miss USA in 1996, not only is she a celebrated beauty pageant titleholder; she is also a notable actress. To name a few of many accomplishments, her acting chops opened a number of prominent doors including a role with an ensemble cast in the sitcom, "Eve" and a part as the Doritos Girl in a 1998 Super Bowl commercial. She went on to appear in similar commercials during the 1998, 1999, and 2000 Super Bowls—no small achievement. Ali has a stack of film and TV roles and has appeared in countless popular productions. Adding to her renown, Ali was named one of 50 most beautiful people in the world by none other than People Magazine. Additionally, she carved out an impressive career modeling early on that laid a solid foundation for her to build her future on. However, her greatest achievement was surrendering her life to the Lord Jesus. I had the privilege of interviewing her in 2023:

INTERVIEW WITH ALI LANDRY:

Ali: All people you know who are faithful have that same question you know we all have that desire for God to show us what's next—like what's our path, where should we go, help us... And sometimes you don't hear His voice right so what you do during that time isn't exactly in keeping with His will, so I love hearing other people's process.

Craig: Yeah, I mean for me too, you know, and you have something to look to, which I love! The question: "I don't know if who am is right?"—that simple question and, "What is my purpose, right?! What am I? Why am I here? I mean we'll ask the same questions. It was Pope John Paul, during World youth he said, "We all search for the meaning of life." And we do! And that question "who am I?" is what moves us, not "what do I do." And Dr. Miles Monroe always asks that question "who am I" and you have that in your book, and I was like—that's so interesting, like if I was to ask you, "Who am I?" yeah, "Who are you Ali" who are you—it's a really hard challenging question; right...

Ali: You know, I think you know those are the big questions in life that we all ponder, right, what I try to present in the book specifically for women I so appreciate that as a man, you asked it too.

Craig: I love it I love it! I don't need to apply makeup, but I love it. And I did, I really did.

Ali: But especially for myself as a mom with kids and a busy morning, I want to set them up for success and share what I've done that really has worked for me. And part of it is, like you mentioned, that morning routine because a lot of times you know we wake up and you feel like it's the Mac Truck of life that hits you, right... The alarm goes off you really want to press snooze, but you don't and it's; go downstairs, make lunches, get the kids going, and then the next thing you know you're diving into work hopefully you could get in a workout, or you know, a quick breakfast.

So, really helping women understand how to set up your morning for success is really important. Part of that time is set aside for prayer and meditation and during that time, like you said, it's that quiet moment, right, it's a time where, for me, it starts with breathing quieting my mind because I'm very Type A and my mind is constantly, constantly racing with the to-do list especially in the morning. It's, you know, it's like what am I going to do? Okay, let me look at the calendar—who is to be picked up, who is to go where, what do I have to do... So just breathing, centering myself, emptying myself out I always am looking at nature like we are right now because that really balances me; puts things into perspective for me because it's God's creation—beauty all around us and focusing on like the little things.

One thing I find with myself, one of my superpowers I will acknowledge is I'm very detailed. I wish people would tell me what I'm sharing, like in the book, I wish they would have explained it to me. That way like even just looking at nature and how to be really present in that moment—what does that even mean? Like, looking out and you're seeing the leaves gently moving as the wind is blowing them or that butterfly that's flying here or there... Do you know, like, to really ground yourself in the present moment because it's very hard to do, right, so, the breathing and then just continually focusing on the breath as the thoughts sort of come in and then trying to find that peace and clarity in my mind. And after I do that for a while, I do always start with a prayer and ask God to fill me up to speak to me in that moment, to fill me up with what He wants me to know and understand and what He wants me to take into my day. Then after that, I will have something to read whether it's the Bible, whether it's some sort of wisdom in a book, whether it's a prayer passage, a daily meditation... And then I journal what was sort of delivered to me and that, now, that's my process of sort of understanding dissecting maybe God's voice and what He wants for me and how to move forward, like in my day.

Craig: I love that, and the routine is so Important.

Ali: But it's taking the time.

Craig: We went away somewhere and during that period, oh it was actually Christmas break, I wasn't you know doing the routine the same way because my son was home, and we were traveling and stuff... But the minute I wasn't sort of doing or fulfilling my routine, I felt sort of disconnected from my faith—yeah right, and then that's when the enemy comes for me, or the voice comes and discouragement, you say "the negative self-talk." And I started finding myself further and further away from, you know, where God was leading me, and I became a little depressed and I got anxious, and I didn't sleep well... Then I realized it was because I wasn't in His Word; same thing—it happened. So, the routine is so important it's not a Sunday thing this isn't like no I build a relationship I go to church once a week. This is every single day, yeah, and you have so many useful tips whether it's food or it's breathing exercises you know everything is in this book it's like a One-Stop shop.

Ali: Well, we really, in the book, yeah, that is definitely a part of it and really helping people understand how to put these routines into your day right that will work for you and serve you. But it's also taking the time to spend with yourself and really explaining or tapping into your heart set—I call it your heart-set, your soul-set, your health-set, and your mindset. And going in to really understand, like what that means, right, like how do you feed your soul? I always say it's when you're doing something right that you're passionate about and you love, and you have that little voice that's saying to you, "Yeah like do more of that that's what you need to do!" Like that's like that's fulfilling your soul, right, bringing in joy to the depths of your being. As adults so often we forget like we stop doing the things we love because life gets busy and other things happen so let's connect with that again, you know, for our health.

As women for myself personally you know I found myself on a daily talk show and I'm here at 5-4-3-2-1—like, live, you know, all cylinders have to be firing. And I was noticing myself on a panel talk show trying to find what I was going to say and I couldn't even connect the dots like the words weren't even coming out. I was like, "Oh gosh I'm gonna lose this gig, like I'm gonna lose this job if I don't figure it out." So, I asked my girlfriends, and they were just kind of like, "Yeah you know that's what happens when we age, or you know we are getting older." And I was like "Wow that doesn't sit well with me like I feel still feel young and I want that vitality in my life, and I want a full healthy life where I'm present and not sitting on the sidelines not feeling my best. So, that's when I dug into my health, right, so the goal is to kind of walk women through how to do that, even your mindset and dealing with social media and comparisons... How to show up for other women and not get engaged in gossip and staying in your lane and do you! You know, life is short that's what I've come to realize—life is short, we have one, so, you got to make it a masterpiece you know or not feeling like halfway there.

INTERVIEW WITH NATASHA BURE, WALK IN FAITH, 2017:

Craig: You spoke about fear in your book, what are you afraid of and how did you overcome it?

Natasha: I'm afraid of heights, I'm afraid of a lot of other things but I'd say my biggest fear is heights. And I think pushing yourself is really important and key, you want to be able to push the boundaries and push the limits and not limit yourself to what you can do just based on your fears. I used to be deathly afraid of heights and wouldn't go on rollercoasters, wouldn't go on any high ropes course or anything like that. I was so afraid and now I do them even if I cry which most of the time I do—I'm bawling my eyes out I can still do it because I just want to prove to myself that I can do it. There's such a cool feeling even after you put yourself through all that misery probably for me like every time I do something like that, I'm like terrified in my heart drops. But it's a, it's a good feeling to know okay I can do it you know I can see exactly!

Craig: When you calm down and just, you know, come to that realization like well what am I really afraid of especially with heights like that's one that I'm sort of afraid of but I did go skydiving to overcome it.

Natasha: You did, what!!!

Craig: Twice; if I go up high in a building, I'm nervous so I went skydiving.

Natasha: No thank you!

Craig: Do you have any weaknesses at all?

Natasha: I'm a very stubborn person, but I think that that can be used as both a weakness and a strength. My mom likes to tell me that, you know, if I'm, if you are stubborn, which I am, like that can obviously be used in a negative way but you can also turn it around.

Craig: Yes, it could be used in a positive way,

Craig: That being said, Natasha do you think that the talents and gifts that God gives us should be used to glorify God?

Natasha: Absolutely to glorify God that is one thing especially just with my love for singing nobody in my family sings and so my mom's like this is definitely God-given talent and I was like I want to use my gift to glorify God and to bring glory to his name and to use a platform that I have you know when I do have a platform to speak about things that are important and you know ultimately to bring praise to Him!

Reflection Questions

- *What specific situations or circumstances trigger feelings of fear in your life?*
- *Try and trace back the origin of your fears to childhood experiences or significant life events?*
- *In what ways do you currently cope with fear, and are these coping mechanisms healthy and effective?*
- *How do your faith and spirituality influence your approach to fear?*
- *What daily spiritual routines and practices can you implement to foster a mindset to overcome and combat fear, negative self-talk, and anxiety.*

CHAPTER FIVE
LEAVING A GODLY LEGACY
REFLECTIONS ON LIFE, LOSS, AND LEAVING A LASTING IMPACT

> *But store up for yourselves treasures in heaven, where moths and vermin do not destroy, and where thieves do not break in and steal. For where your treasure is, there your heart will be also.*
> —*Matthew 6:20-21 (NIV)*

As I approach the final chapter, I pray that this book has provided some inspiration for you and hasn't merely become a decorative prop on your nightstand, I must admit that I started writing this book during the initial stages of the pandemic. It provided not just the time but a clear perspective on my life or so I thought. Much has changed since then, and I believe God wanted me to pause before writing this last chapter on "legacy."

And as I did, I couldn't help but reflect on the incredible individuals I've had the privilege of interviewing. It occurred to me, within my spirit, that I should have a conversation with my good friend Joe Estevez, a highly successful actor with over 300 productions under his belt. Joe hosted a show I produced called "All Things Catholic" and played a priest in a film I wrote and directed called "Omerta." He is also the younger brother of Martin Sheen and uncle to Emilio Estevez and Charlie Sheen. While on my way to Los Angeles for a spiritual retreat, I called Joe, informed him about my book, and asked if we could meet and chat for a few hours. During our time together, we delved into his life, career, and the impact he hopes to make on his children, family, and everyone he encounters. Our conversation covered a wide range of topics, from his addiction to his spiritual journey, to his relationship with his brother and his personal health and legacy. While I couldn't include the entire interview in this book, I believe this portion of our conversation reflects his perspective on the importance and power of legacy and that it will inspire you, just as it has inspired me.

INTERVIEW WITH JOE ESTEVEZ:

Craig: What would your kids say about the legacy that you will be leaving behind? Because it won't be your book or your movies. What will be your legacy?

Joe: You know, basically... In a word, love. And to love deeply. And to love unconditionally. Which I don't think... In the last 30-35 years, I've been able to do that. I was broken. I was... This is back when I was living up on Hollymon up here. And I was doing some things... I was doing a lot of things I shouldn't be doing.

Craig: Such as?

Joe: I was doing drugs. I was spending all my money. I was working a lot. But I was spending whatever I made for things that were feeding my habit. And I wasn't being the father that I should have been to my children. I wasn't being the human being I should have been to my God. Every night... I prayed. I still do, every night. And I always said, "Yeah, I'm gonna beat this. I'm gonna beat this. I know I can beat this..." And then... Finally, it beat me, and I admitted that I need help, I can't do this. I can't—it's got me. And it's gonna kill me. You know?

Craig: Did you ever contemplate suicide?

Joe: No, no. I've never in my darkest world. And when I gave up drinking, even though I was doing these other things... I never drank. But to tell the story again, I woke up about four o'clock in the morning. And it's glorious. And it's indescribable. And I've tried to describe it. It's indescribable. There are no words. There are no... But it was...The Spirit of the Holy... The Holy Spirit just... It was enrapturing. It was just... joy. Utter and complete joy. Love. Utter love. Peace. Goodness. I was being embraced. I was loved so much. I was so precious. I was so wanted. I was so good. I was... I woke up... Tears pouring down. Smiling. My arms up in the air. Thank you, thank you, thank you, thank you. Since July of 1974, I've either jogged or walked every day. But... I hadn't done it for a couple of months. I was heavy. I was a mess. I got on my bed, my arms in the air. And... I jogged through the... Hills in Hollywood up here. It was just... Thank you, thank you, thank you, thank you. All the... Everything I did. All the addiction had—gone... Just gone. Taken from me. Just gone. In this rapture. It was just gone. It was there. And I was with it. And... Running through the hills. And it was during... Lent. So, the churches were open. And I must have been up on those hills. Three-and-a-half, or four hours. I just, I was just bawling with joy. Just in tears. And... I would go, and... I'd sit in a Catholic church. And... The folks thought I was weeping. Because of the way of the cross and Jesus dying—I was weeping with joy, man. But that was the only place I felt safe.

Craig: That is a such a powerful story, I've heard similar stories from people that I have interviewed and had a serious addiction and were losing control of their lives and right when they were close to giving up hope they called out to God, and He intervened, and they were saved from the stronghold of the addiction. How did that experience or awakening shape the advice that you offer fellow actors?

Joe: I used to speak at film festivals, and they'd ask me to talk about actors and the art of being an actor. I would like to inspire these kids and these actors, by the art of acting. Not the art of trying to be a star or the art of trying to make money, but the art of acting. And what a marvelous art that is—it's a gift that you've been given to by God, and God did not put that passion in your heart by accident. There's a purpose for it to be there, I don't think that it's for money or for fame. It's for help. To put out into the world. Maybe with that, I've inspired some people. Maybe. Maybe not. I don't know if I left them a legacy, I can say that I've helped, and I know I've helped my three children. And that even when I was broken, it has always been total unconditional love. I've never even thought about hitting them. If I get angry with them, I hug them. Oh, hey, come on, man, come on, you know, and they wouldn't do it again because they didn't want me to make me feel bad, you know. But I think with them and just that knowing those children, knowing that unconditional love that I gave them and that unconditional love, it comes from God through me.

Craig: What would you say your legacy will be? Do you have any regrets at all? I know you said, you were hooked on meth and drugs and alcohol, but what regrets do you have and what would you say to someone younger as they're trying to build a legacy, not based on money and fame, but a legacy, like unconditional love? What would you say to them?

Joe: Learn who you are. Learn as best you can who you really are. I love that word, retreat, think about and let it penetrate you about what you're doing here as a human being. About the power and the glory and the majesty that is, is you, is within you. That beauty that is so undefinable. You know, I bow to the God within, I bow to the God within you. You know, that, I see that in you guys. I hope that my children, my family and the people on the street and the people that I do theater with and the people that I come in contact with every day, that they see that peace in me, and they want that peace. And I think maybe if I've left that as a legacy... If I can put out that positive vibration out there, I've been incredibly blessed. I don't know what else to do besides what I'm doing to leave a legacy. My job is to gain wisdom and peace and love and goodness.

Craig: Joe how would define success? Are you successful?

Joe: Being an actor is a pathway to that if you use it correctly, you know? Being at peace. In a word, being at peace. And that peace incorporates love. Peace—peace! Not to worry about making the rent or my car payment. And I'm not there, you know? I have peace in my heart, but I'm still human and I still have frailties. But to attain peace, to enjoy peace. You know, I heard that somebody said, "Man, this guy, you know, he took Jesus Christ literally. You know, you're not supposed to..." Well, how else are you supposed to take it, you know? When that guy, you know, came to Jesus, and said, I want to follow you, Jesus said, that's great, man. Give away all that you own and join the club. He said, I will. I'll get back to you on that. Yeah, yeah. He said, where's your faith? You know, your faith can move mountains. You know, if you believe it, it's true. You have to believe it. Tough as that, you know? So, I think for me, I like to just be able to step out in spirit. Because I believe in it. You know, I'm a vessel, you know? I'm just unmitigated love. I'm unmitigated peace. I'm joy. I'm joy! And that's who I am! It's gotten so materialistic that these kids don't even realize that there's a spiritual side to them. They think, "What more can I get? What better car, what better apartment?" And, you know; the commercialism pushes that. You know, and this is going to make it happen. And it's so far away about who we are and how misguided this society and most all societies are. You know? I think that I don't know how much longer this can keep going the way it is before there's a revolution or a reckoning to where people come back and realize it themselves.

Craig: Your right, I mean, the commercialism, materialism, this whole fixated focus on themselves and what social media and society says will bring happiness. So, what advice would you give to them?

> *Joe: It's what I said before. Find out who you are. Find out who you are naked. Find out who you are without any accoutrements. See that person that is you without the jewels, or the cars, or the clothes... Who is that person? Because that's ultimately your work here is discover that glory in you and pass it on as a legacy. So, I think we all have that legacy in us but we all, only a few of us realize that and practice it.*

Though we are all finding our footing again after the cruelty and fallout of the Coronavirus disease at this juncture in our history, I don't want to dwell on how the pandemic has affected my life and the world in which we live. I believe we've all experienced the challenges Covid-19 presented in various ways; so instead, I'll focus on the recent shifts in my life.

As I reflect on this crucial chapter, I must share that my father unexpectedly passed away from an infection. His passing has added a profound layer to my understanding of legacy. My father's passing was abrupt; no goodbyes, no preparations, he was taken to the hospital and passed away only a few hours later. My sister and I were on our way to the hospital to see him when we got the call that he died. In that moment, I sensed that God was preparing me for this, enabling me to be a source of strength for my family. Gratefully, I embraced that role.

As I grappled with this loss, I found solace in holding onto my rosary beads, repeatedly reciting, "I put my faith and trust in the Lord." It brought me strength and comfort during these challenging times. The night before his passing, I woke up in tears and had this profound sense that my dad had left us, it was as if God was preparing me for what I was about to experience.

My sister was very adamant about seeing my father one last time, despite his passing, I chose to wait for her in the car, just praying and reflecting until my family arrived.

I witnessed the enduring impact my father had on my brother, who swiftly and unhesitatingly assumed the responsibilities of caring for our mother, just as our father had done for the past 60 years of his life. It seemed as though there was no interruption in the flow of love and care; she was looked after with the same devotion as my father once did.

My brother continues to exemplify this unconditional love towards our mother, and this invaluable lesson is being passed on to his children as they witness the compassion he extends to their grandmother. These are teachings that go beyond words, emphasizing the importance of actions. Through his actions, my brother is instilling in his children a godly legacy, much like the one my father cultivated within us.

This attribute of unconditional love is a quality that is within all of us, not just a selected few, and we are called to imitate Christ by showing love to all creation, especially our parents; and I am certain our father is watching from above and is incredibly proud of my brother.

I won't delve into the details of the following days, as we've all encountered the loss of a loved one, and the pain that follows can be hard to bear. Some of us concentrate on the immediate days, immersing ourselves in activities as a way of distraction, while others choose moments of quiet reflection.

> "Not everyone who says to me, 'Lord, Lord,' will enter the kingdom of heaven, but the one who does the will of my Father who is in heaven. On that day many will say to me, 'Lord, Lord, did we not prophesy in your name, and cast out demons in your name, and do many mighty works in your name?' And then will I declare to them, 'I never knew you; depart from me, you workers of lawlessness.'"
> Matthew 7:21-23

I chose to spend the next few days reflecting on my father's life, and although my father was a good man who believed in God and the Kingdom of heaven, I feared that he lacked a personal relationship with Jesus Christ and I'm familiar with Mathew 7:21-7:23, "Not everyone who says to me, 'Lord, Lord,' will enter the kingdom of heaven, but the one who does the will of my Father who is in heaven. On that day many will say to me, 'Lord, Lord, did we not prophesy in your name, and cast out demons in your name, and do many mighty works in your name?' And then will I declare to them, 'I never knew you; depart from me, you workers of lawlessness.'"

I couldn't shake the thought that I might not see him again because he lacked a personal relationship with Jesus Christ. Even though he was a good man, he wasn't necessarily a godly man. So, I prayed earnestly, asking God to forgive him and welcome him into His Kingdom and into eternal peace, hoping we would reunite in heaven.

I wish I could say that God spoke to me, assuring me of my prayer. However, He remained silent, and there were no extraordinary signs. Yet, something did happen, something I was not expecting.

Before I go any further, I want to explain and define the word "legacy": *Legacy: a gift by will especially of money or other personal property: bequest.*[1] The term "Legacy" holds both a secular and spiritual perspective. Secularly, it refers to an inheritance, involving an amount of money or property left in a will. In this context, it centers on the material aspects associated with someone's passing, such as receiving assets for personal use like vacations or home improvements.

On the spiritual front, Legacy takes on a deeper meaning. It encompasses the enduring impact of past events, actions, or an individual's life. This spiritual legacy transcends generations, passing down invaluable lessons to our children's children, contributing to a priceless and spiritually enriching heritage that pays spiritual dividends. You can see this in Proverbs 13:22, "A good man leaves an inheritance to his children's children." I believe that the inheritance he is referring to is not solely based in material possessions, but a spiritual heritage that defines the identity, character, and intimacy with God.

> "A good man leaves an inheritance to his children's children."
> Proverbs 13:22

During the wake, I continued to struggle with my father's final resting place, but then I met colleagues and friends that shared stories about how my father had impacted their lives. It was then that I learned about his acts of kindness, his support, and the love he had shown to so many people. I was unaware of these stories, but as they unfolded in conversations, I became immediately captivated. Our neighbor expressed gratitude to my mother, sharing how my father assisted him in securing a job at his workplace and even helped him acquire the house next door to ours. Another friend recounted how my dad supported him at work and was always there whenever he needed assistance. Throughout the day, I continued to learn about more instances where my father played a crucial role in helping and positively influencing the lives of many. These stories painted a portrait of a man who left a legacy not defined by wealth or property but by the love and care he had given and shown to others.

The following day was the funeral, and I feared they might request that I speak about my father. Fortunately, I had prepared some notes, but to my relief, my sister took the initiative to share some thoughts about our dad. She was followed by his niece, also my godmother, who spoke about how my father consistently supported and assisted her. She eloquently conveyed the deep love he had for his family and friends, emphasizing his willingness to help anyone in need.

It was astonishing to discover these stories about the man I referred to as my father—my dad, my abba. My sister also shared how my father would drive and, pick her up, and they would enjoy pizza together, simply spending quality time. Additionally, she highlighted his consistent concern, always asking if she needed anything during their conversations.

Tears streamed down my face as I came to the realization that he was in heaven, and God would welcome him. Despite not fitting the textbook definition of a Christian or maintaining a daily relationship with Jesus Christ, my father embodied the works of Jesus by loving people and assisting everyone he encountered, regardless of his circumstances.

I doubt my father comprehended the impact or legacy he was leaving, but those who encountered him spoke of what they received from him—his love, humor, friendship, faith, devotion, and his smile. He left a legacy that will live on for generations to come.

It continues to get easier as the days progress, yet what I miss most is being unable to call him and say hello and tell him about my day because he always told me how proud he was of me and my accomplishments; that would help me press on and continue another day. It can be hard doing what we do; the world doesn't always accept us or our way of thinking, and he reminded me of the good I was doing even when others would come against me.

I often reflect on the godly legacy my father left me. When I face moments of doubt or struggle, I remember that one man with humble means can achieve great impact, influencing many with simple acts of love and kindness. If my father could accomplish this without recognition until his passing, I can draw strength to press on through the pain and adversity, whether internal or external.

I've always been someone who delves into profound thoughts and enjoys engaging in such conversations. Before my father's passing, I contemplated writing my own obituary from the perspective of a loved one. What would they write, and what would they say about the impact, if any, that I've made? I pondered what I'd be known and remembered for—whether it would be akin to a life insurance policy or how I affected their lives. Would they say I lived a life resembling Jesus or one mirroring society, what would they say?

I frequently contemplate these matters, and when I delve into reflection, anything that doesn't align with Christ or that I'm not proud of, I strive to remove from my life. Our calling is to be a reflection of Christ, working towards holiness, and anything contradictory requires our attention for elimination. My aspiration is for people to say to my son and my wife, "Your father or your husband was there for me, inspired me toward Christ, and helped me in ways that brought positive change to my life." I desire my life to have meaning for them—a means to change and impact other people's lives, drawing them into a closer relationship with Jesus Christ.

I aspire for my legacy to mirror my father's legacy, impacting and inspiring numerous people through the love we extend to God's children, our brothers, and sisters. What continues to amaze me about my father's legacy is that I was unaware of how he influenced countless individuals through his actions, words, and deeds; at times my father lived Matthew 6:3-4, "But when you give to the needy, do not let your left hand know what your right hand is doing, so that your giving may be in secret. And your Father who sees in secret will reward you." In today's world, it's challenging to live out the passage because everything is broadcasted through social media and YouTube. I believe that God is blessing me because of the life my father lived.

> Matthew 6:3-4, "But when you give to the needy, do not let your left hand know what your right hand is doing, so that your giving may be in secret. And your Father who sees in secret will reward you."

My father didn't make preparations for his departure; he didn't have a will or any final arrangements in place. Often, we get caught up in thinking about what material possessions, like life insurance policies or properties, we'll leave for our children to secure their survival or success. However, we overlook what is truly important and what will outlast material wealth—the impact we make through living a life that reflects Jesus Christ and showing our family how much we love and care for them.

Promoting love and dignity for all, teaching forgiveness, respecting, and honoring extended families and friends, adhering to God's standards rather than society's, praying, and putting trust and faith in God and His Word—this is the legacy I speak of. It's a legacy that will not only change and impact your life but also influence those around you. If we could all take one thing from my father, it would be that you don't need wealth to leave a legacy or to impact someone's life or to love someone unconditionally. If we collectively strive to live lives reflecting the works of Jesus Christ, regardless of hostility or persecution, we can work towards changing the world and instilling the values of our faith, which is unconditional love.

I am extremely grateful to my father for teaching me valuable lessons on being a good father and emphasizing the significance of leaving a legacy. I also thank God for unveiling insights that were not apparent to me over the years but were revealed at the right time. Additionally, I am thankful for the assurance that I will reunite with my father, and upon his arrival at the gate, God will welcome him with the words from Matthew 25:23, "Well done, good and faithful servant!"

It brings me great comfort to acknowledge this, as I have encountered numerous affluent individuals who dedicate their lives to preparing and accumulating wealth for their eventual passing, only to leave behind nothing that is enduring or spiritually enriching. Material possessions and financial assets will fade away over time, but the enduring love we extend to others will resonate eternally.

A few years ago, I was filming a commercial for a cemetery, and we encountered one of the largest crypts I've ever seen. The man, who was still alive, had invested over a million dollars in its construction, and he said jokingly that he wanted to include an ATM machine, so that his family would visit him after he passed. What kind of legacy is that? It's certainly not the one I intend to leave behind, and I encourage you to consider a different perspective. If there's one thing to take away from this book, it's that I am here today because of the spiritual legacy passed down by my grandparents and my father. I'm not extraordinary; I'm just someone who discovered what God was calling me to do and continues to pursue it despite obstacles or adversity and continues to live out this passage in Proverbs 18:16, "A man's gift makes room for him, and brings him before great men" (NKJV). The key is not me but my gifts which come from God and it's my job to develop those gifts and use them to glorify God and His Kingdom.

As I write this thought, my Alexa decided to play Frank Sinatra's "Send in the Clowns." The words from this song were echoed at my father's funeral, my father did it his way, another confirmation that he is with me.

> Proverbs 18:16, "A man's gift makes room for him, and brings him before great men" (NKJV).

In times of loss, our faith undergoes testing, and the choice to lean on God and deepen our faith becomes crucial. Personally, I not only relied on my faith but also on my family. My father's passing has drawn my siblings and me closer together as we now share a common bond—caring for and comforting our mother. Surprisingly, my father's departure has also brought family and friends closer in ways I couldn't have foreseen during his lifetime. Cousins are now requesting one of his old sweatshirts or neckties just to feel his presence and reflect on the impact he had on their lives. Recently, my mother revealed that my father often wondered who, if anyone, would attend his funeral and what they would say about him. He questioned whether his life had meaning, measuring success by the impact he made and the legacy he aspired to leave behind.

Even in the twilight of his life, after all the good he had done, the people he had helped, and the inspiration he had provided, he still harbored doubts about being loved and whether his life held meaning. I made a point to express my love for him as often as possible, acknowledging his greatness as a father. Looking back, I realize I should have done this more during my upbringing. Perhaps I should have thanked him for taking me to basketball practice or karate class. Instead, I took it for granted and even complained when he went straight from work, wearing his work clothes, embarrassing me. I failed to see that his mere presence should have sufficed. He never complained about taking me, always encouraged me, and cheered me on. Now I understand the sacrifices he made for me. His consistent presence left an enduring impression on me. At the time, I failed to appreciate it fully, and I wish I had been more grateful. The love and presence he showed me mirror the love Jesus demonstrated to everyone he encountered. It's a love I carry from my father, now transferred to my son, Mario.

My faith in Jesus Christ and His Word sustains me through this challenging time, and I find solace in the seemingly small signs or "winks" from God. As I mentioned earlier, I don't believe in coincidences. While in route to film an episode of "Walk in Faith," I heard a word in my spirit and then I spoke it aloud, "I feel closer to my father now than I did before, and he is in heaven." Reflecting on it, I sensed an unprecedented closeness and even felt a profound peace wash over me.

After we finished filming the interviews, we decided to go out for lunch, and during our goodbyes, the priest I had interviewed approached me and expressed a desire to pray for me and my father. Welcoming the blessing, especially for my father, I felt his hand on my shoulder as he echoed the exact words, "Your father is closer to you now than before, and he is in heaven." Overwhelmed with emotion, I cried, recognizing that God was speaking through him. There was no way he could have known what I heard in my spirit while driving alone in my car. I thanked him for the blessing, realizing that even a humble man like Sonny continued to impact not only my life and those who knew him but also this priest whom I had just met. Hearing those words reassured me, dispelling any doubts about my father lacking a personal relationship with Jesus Christ. It also eradicated any fear that God might not welcome him into His Kingdom. Instead, I believe God would say, "Well done, my good and faithful servant."

I express gratitude to God for guiding me through the profound experience of discovering who my father truly was and the enduring impact his life continues to have on numerous people. A humble man named Sonny, leading an ordinary life, yet creating an extraordinary impact. If he could achieve such influence, just imagine the possibilities for what we can do with the resources at our disposal.

Now, I can confidently affirm that my father has left an indelible mark on my life, surpassing the impact of anyone I have ever encountered. While I have met many individuals, who have achieved great and remarkable successes, my father gave me the most significant legacy—a godly one. My only regret is not expressing gratitude more frequently during my upbringing. Don't wait until it's too late to honor and appreciate those who shape your life. Extend your gratitude while they are still present; if I had done so earlier, my father might not have questioned the significance of his life or whether his actions truly influenced others, as I could have provided reassurance.

I witnessed the profound impact my father has had on my son. At just eight-years-old, my son displays remarkable emotional maturity, love, compassion, and wisdom. It underscores the idea that children possess more intelligence than we often give them credit for, especially when we encourage open communication.

Recently, my son was moved to tears because he longed for one more conversation with my father. While he understands that Grandpa is in heaven, he longs for another chance to express his love. My father had a unique way of showering him with love and expressing pride in him. Although we consistently reassure our son of our love throughout the day, there's something distinct about the unconditional love a grandfather provides. The impact my father had on my son continues to radiate through the cracks of his grieving heart.

It was heart-wrenching to witness, as I empathize with his feelings—I, too, would give anything for one more acknowledgment of pride from my father. Those reminders are invaluable, and I am grateful for the times my father expressed how proud he was of me.

This legacy now influences how I speak words of faith and love over my son and wife. My father's impact extends far and wide and seeing it through my son's eyes is a testament to the singular power that one man can have over many.

It serves as a reminder of the influence that we all possess, a power that can either build up our family and friends or tear them down. My father chose to reflect the qualities of Christ by building people up rather than tearing them down.

One of my father's cherished songs was "The Living Years" by Mike + the Mechanics, and I regret not paying closer attention to the lyrics when he sang them to me. Looking back now, I believe the lyrics resonated with him, reflecting the strained relationship he had with his own father. Singing those words to me stirred deep emotions within him, I hope you'll take a moment to listen to this powerful song:

The Living Years
By: B.A. Robertson and Mike Rutherford
(As Recorded by Mike + the Mechanics)

Every generation
Blames the one before
And all of their frustrations
Come beating on your door
I know that I'm a prisoner
To all my Father held so dear
I know that I'm a hostage
To all his hopes and fears
I just wish I could have told him in the living years

Oh, crumpled bits of paper
Filled with imperfect thoughts
Stilted conversations
I'm afraid that's all we've got

You say you just don't see it
He says it's perfect sense
You just can't get agreement
In this present tense
We all talk a different language
Talking in defense

Say it loud (say it loud), say it clear (oh, say it clear)
You can listen as well as you hear, yeah
It's too late (it's too late) when we die (oh, when we die)
To admit we don't see eye to eye

So we open up a quarrel
Between the present and the past
We only sacrifice the future
It's the bitterness that lasts
So don't yield to the fortunes
You sometimes see as fate
It may have a new perspective
On a different day
And if you don't give up, and don't give in
You may just be okay

So say it, say it, say it loud, say it clear (oh, say it clear)
You can listen as well as you hear
Because it's too late, it's too late (it's too late)
When we die (oh, when we die)
To admit we don't see eye to eye

I wasn't there that morning
When my Father passed away
I didn't get to tell him
All the things I had to say
I think I caught his spirit

Later that same year
I'm sure I heard his echo
In my baby's new born tears
I just wish I could have told him in the living years

So say it, say it, say it loud, say it clear (oh, say it clear)
You can listen as well as you hear, yeah
It's too late (it's too late) when we die (it's too late when we die)
To admit we don't see eye to eye

Hey, so say it, say it, say it loud (say it loud, say it loud)
Say it clear (come on say it clear)
Say it loud
(Don't give up, don't give in and don't look away 'til it's too late)
Say it clear)[2]

I hope these lyrics from one of my father's favorite songs will also inspire you to "Say it Loud, and say it clear, I love you."

You are in my prayers, and I kindly ask for your prayers for me and my father, Salvatore "Sonny" Tubiolo, a remarkable man who left behind a legacy that I will continue to share in everyone's life.

As a final thought, I would like to share a few Bible passages to help you shape and contemplate the legacy you wish to leave behind. Don't postpone this reflection until later in life, start thinking about it now. If you're open to my suggestion, consider writing your own obituary or seek assistance from a friend. Reflect on the insights that emerge and begin taking stock of aspects in your life that can be altered or eliminated. Avoid becoming overly preoccupied with societal standards, as such preoccupations serve as distractions from the enemy, and comparison is one of Satan's tools of diversion from God's plan for your life. And when you experience challenging times, which are inevitable, repeat these simple words, "I put my faith and trust in the Lord, I put my faith and trust in the Lord." These simple words can assist you in overcoming fear and adversity.

While there are many more, a few Bible passages to meditate on as you shape your legacy include:

- Ephesians 6.4: "Fathers, do not exasperate your children; instead, bring them up in the training and instruction of the Lord" (NIV).
- Deuteronomy 6.5-7: "You shall love the LORD your God with all your heart and with all your soul and with all your might. And these words that I command you today shall be on your heart. You shall teach them diligently to your children, and shall talk of them when you sit in your house, and when you walk by the way, and when you lie down, and when you rise."
- Psalm 145.4: "One generation shall commend your works to another, and shall declare your mighty acts."
- 1 Peter 4.10: "Each of you should use whatever gift you have received to serve others, as faithful stewards of God's grace in its various forms" (NIV).

Bishop T.D. Jakes' insight and command of the Bible has impacted millions worldwide, guiding them into a deeper and more personal relationship with Jesus Christ. And though I haven't had the opportunity to meet or interview Bishop Jakes, his impactful words and vision as a man of God continue to shape my spiritual journey. If you're unfamiliar with him or The Potter's House, I recommend taking the time to listen to his powerful messages. While I don't recall where I heard or read this profound observation by Bishop Jakes, it has resonated with me for a long time and I'd like to share this meaningful quote from him, "Your legacy is every life you've touched. And those you've touched will touch others. That's the most lasting legacy of all."

We should all work towards creating the type of legacy that will continue to impact long after our time has passed as Psalm 89:1 urges us, "I will sing of the steadfast love of the Lord, forever; with my mouth I will make known your faithfulness to all generations." Bishop T.D. Jakes' words ring true in my life—from my father, who left a godly legacy, to all the people I've met who have impacted my spiritual journey.

Bishop T.D. Jakes, I eagerly anticipate the day when I can sit across from you for an interview and express how profoundly you've influenced my life. This quote perfectly encapsulates the legacy of an ordinary man with an extraordinary heart, named Salvatore or "Sonny," who happened to be my father.

---

1. Merriam-Webster.com Dictionary, s.v. "legacy," accessed February 2, 2024, https://www.merriam-webster.com/dictionary/legacy.
2. LyricFind. Robertson, B.A., Rutherford, Mike. 'The Living Years', 1989. https://lyrics.lyricfind.com/lyrics/mike-the-mechanics-the-living-years. Accessed February 5, 2024.

EPILOGUE

As I pour out the last of my heart, my earnest prayer is that my words have stirred inspiration or left an impact, guiding you toward the discovery of God's plan for your life and revealing what lies beneath the surface. I've always been intrigued by self-examination, personal improvement, and growth, and this fascination led me to pursue a certification as a Christian life coach.

Throughout my career I've read numerous books and conducted extensive research, finding myself apprehended by a recurring theme. While motivational speakers possessed an impressive body of insightful, thought-provoking knowledge and wisdom, a crucial element seemed absent—Jesus Christ. To truly experience transformation and fulfillment, a relationship with Jesus Christ is essential. Most of what I was hearing and what the motivational speakers were motivating people with was more about feeding the flesh than feeding the spirit.

It was this insight that inspired me to pack the pages you're turning, with the knowledge gained through my certification process and experiences as the host of "Walk in Faith." My goal is to share insights from the perspective of God's plan for our lives rather than our own.

My intentions are not to boast or brag about who I have met or interviewed but to act as a conduit, sharing insights to help at least one person. Recognizing God's prompting in my heart, witnessing this journey come to fruition, and glimpsing the finish line fills me with immense gratitude. The path has not been easy or straightforward, but it has served as a reminder of God's unwavering love and the blessings bestowed upon me.

I understand that what I ask of you is neither easy nor swift; like the caterpillar cloistered in its cocoon awaiting its wings, the transformation takes time. Please, do not be discouraged or give up, for God will persistently knock until you answer. I have endeavored to lay out what I've learned through my faith journey and interactions with people who have profoundly impacted my life. Consider those in your own life who inspire and speak into your spirit, and if none come to mind, turn to our heavenly Father, for He will never disappoint or abandon you. There is much more I desire to share—from my youth in Brooklyn to my later days working in the church. My faith has been tested, the enemy has been in my presence, I have witnessed the power of the Holy Spirit and have felt the presence of God in my life. Although there were moments when it seemed tempting to quit, something always propelled me forward, prompting me to give it one more day.

Committing to Jesus Christ and cultivating a daily relationship is not easy, and not all of us will attain riches and fame like some of my guests. However, I can assure you the joy, fulfillment, and spiritual wealth that bring the meaningful life available to all who commit and come to Jesus Christ. I have experienced this personally, along with my guests.

When my guests committed their lives to Jesus Christ, doors opened, leading to a transformed life through a daily relationship with Him. From my experiences, I've learned that countless individuals underwent a transformative journey when they identified their gifts, which, in turn, led them to their purpose. Through a daily relationship with Jesus Christ, God unveiled His plan, resulting in a profound transformation in their lives.

This theme is echoed in the majority of my interviews and serves as the key to your success and legacy. Spend some time watching "Walk in Faith" to hear how the lives of individuals like Mark Wahlberg and his brother Jim were transformed by the power of the Holy Spirit.

Let me emphasize that this is not a Sunday-only thing; it's a daily relationship that needs development. You don't have to join a church to initiate this relationship; you only need to let God know you are ready to listen to what He has been whispering in your spirit all these years. He has been patiently waiting for you to welcome Him into your life, and I assure you, once you do, your life will never be the same. I wasn't always "Catholic Craig" or the host of "Walk in Faith." I was once a depressed lonely kid who was lost and searching for significance and acceptance. Through the power, grace, and love of Jesus Christ, I am here today with a passion and fire to share my story and God's love for all His children, regardless of color, race, gender, or creed. I hope that you will also be inspired to share the knowledge and experience in this book with all that you meet and interact with because we are called in Matthew 28:19-20 "Go therefore and make disciples of all nations, baptizing them in the name of the Father and of the Son and of the Holy Spirit, teaching them to observe all things that I have commanded you..."

I will continue to pray for you and your journey. Feel free to reach out to me, as I was once like you, searching for answers while God was right there waiting for me to welcome Him into my heart. Never lose hope or question your worth; those are the lies of the enemy. Repeat these words from Psalm 139:14, "I am fearfully and wonderfully made." And always remember that God loves you unconditionally and we are all brothers and sisters in Christ.

"Always remember, you have the ability to inspire and evangelize through your words and actions."

Craig Syracusa
Brooklyn, NY
2/15/2024

PHOTOS

Attending a family wedding with my beautiful wife, Dana, and my handsome son, Mario

Celebrating Christmas with my In-laws in 2023

Celebrating Msgr. Cassato's 50th Jubilee with my family

Celebrating my niece Grace's communion in 2021 with my gorgeous wife, Dana, and my handsome son, Mario

Conducting an Interview with Mark Wahlberg for the film Father Stu

Enjoying my neice Grace's communion in 2021 with my family

Interviewing Greg Kinnear, Renee Zellweger, and Djimon Hounsou for the film, Same Kind of Different

Going to dinner with my son, Mario

Interviewing actor, Jim Caviezel for the film, Paul

Mario, spending time with his Grandpa

Msgr. Jamie, Lou Sandoval (who is the artsist), and myself are presenting Alejandro and his wife Ali Landry with a statue in L.A.

On set, filming an episode of Walk in Faith

My interview with Gaston Pauls for the film, Palau

On the Red Carpet conducting interviews for Entertainment Tonight, Canada

Spending quality time with my son, Mario

Visiting the Vatican in 2023

ACKNOWLEDGMENTS

I want to offer my deepest appreciation to all those who have stood by me throughout my journey of faith, in a sense they rode shotgun for me through both the highs and lows.

To my grandparents, Mary and Michael, who showed me unconditional love and helped shape and mold my faith in Jesus Christ.

To my mother, Phyllis, who insisted on taking me to church during my upbringing and remains one of my biggest supporters, showering me with love and kindness.

To my father and friend Sonny who I know is looking down on me, he taught me how to be a dad and left behind the most incredible gift—a godly legacy.

To my siblings and their children, who I love, and treasure the time we share.

Gratitude extends to my in-laws, who have embraced me as part of their family and continue loving me with all my flaws and my odd sense of humor.

You are my rock—my wife, partner, and best friend who has always supported my lifestyle, creativity, ideas, and the challenges of being a communicator for Christ.

My son Mario, who I love more than words could ever express, he is my angel, my buddy, my love, my reason, my why; I pray that my efforts and commitment to our family, our faith, and you will leave a lasting impact on your life, just as my father's influence shaped mine.

I can't forget our dog Brownie, who is always by my feet when I'm home working.

I want to give a special thanks to all the guests and friends I've interviewed, sharing stories and testimonials and our shared journey of faith.

I also want to thank Carl Dobrowolski and his team at Goodwill Rights Management, who helped me throughout this process; this book would not have been possible without the love that Carl and his team showed me.

I also want to thank Msgr. Jamie and Msgr. Cassato for their spiritual guidance and friendship throughout the years.

Above all, I express my deepest gratitude to God, my Lord and Savior. His grace, love, and forgiveness have sustained me, and even in moments of ignorance, He persistently pursued me until I finally surrendered. I commit to continue being a communicator for Christ, sharing His story and how it has impacted my life with as many people as possible, knowing that if He could save and transform my life, He can do the same for you.

www.ingramcontent.com/pod-product-compliance
Lightning Source LLC
LaVergne TN
LVHW061529070526
838199LV00009B/433